GAMEPLAN will be a helpful addition to any high school athlete's daily routine. Collin understands the mind of a high school athlete and has structured the devotions in such a way that they can be useful for whatever situation each individual is currently facing. For any high school athlete seeking to integrate their faith with their sport, GAMEPLAN will meet you where you're at—and help guide you toward the path that God has laid out for you.

– Brian Smith, author of *The Christian Athlete*

A KINGDOM APPROACH TO SPORTS

GAME PLAN

101 Devotions for High School Athletes

Foreword by Olympian Ryan Hall

COLLIN OSWALT

COMET
TALE
BOOKS

To Jesus Christ, Who gave His life to save mine.
(2 Corinthians 5:14–15)

TABLE OF CONTENTS

A Word from an Olympian...xi

The Big Question xiii

Note to the Reader... xv

Read This First 1

PRESEASON.. **4**

Starting a New Season 5

Remembering Your Identity 7

Getting a New Coach 9

After a Summer Weights Session.. 11

Talking Faith with Teammates 13

Ordering Sports Gear... 15

During Summer Training Camp 17

Purifying Your Playlist 19

Kick-Starting Spiritual Growth............................... 21

Saying No to Peer Pressure 23

Breaking Free from People Pleasing....................... 25

Setting Season Goals 27

Finding a Role Model 29

Surrendering Social Media...................................... 31

Struggling to Trust God.. 33

Stressed Out... 35

Beginning of the School Year.................................. 37

Using Your Time Wisely.. 39

Maximizing Your Gifts.. 41

Finding True Satisfaction 43

PRACTICE..**46**

First Practice 47

Learning the Playbook 49

Start of a New Week 51

Hard Day at Practice 53

After a Morning Practice................................... 55

Mid-Season Boredom 57

Making Sacrifices.. 59

Facing the Fear of Others 61

Feeling Discouraged 63

Going Through a Trial... 65

Convicted Over Sin 67

Standing Up Against Bullying.......................... 69

Frustrated with a Teammate............................. 71

Burdened Beyond Bearing 73

Missed a Practice 75

Feeling Stuck In Your Routine 77

Getting Home from Practice 79

Serving Your Teammates 81

Watching Your Words... 83

Sharing the Gospel 85

Needing Inspiration.. 87

Resisting Temptation 89

Following a Film Session.................................... 91

Unhappy with Your Circumstances.................. 93

Staying on Your Guard.. 95

PRE-COMPETITION **98**

Kicking Off the Season 99

Maintaining a Proper Perspective 101

Riding the Bus...103

Lacking Motivation 105

Waiting to Compete 107

Night Before Competing 109

Facing Your Toughest Opponent 111

Feeling Pressure to Perform 113

Trash Talking 115

Preparing for the Postseason 117

Competing with Excellence 119

Focusing on Christ 121

Completely Overwhelmed 123

Your Most Important Competition 125

Competing for What Counts 127

POST-COMPETITION **130**

Fell Short of Winning 131

Knowing What to Say 133

Battling Pride 135

Won an Upset 137

The Morning After Competing 139

A Record was Broken 141

Assessing Your Actions 143

Conquering Envy 145

Frustrated with the Season 147

After a Hard Loss 149

Responding to Adversity 151

Silencing Comparison 153

Confessing Sin 155

Came Down to the Wire 157

Encountering Crisis 159

Made a Big Mistake 161

Responding to Praise 163

Disheartened by Defeat...165

Things Aren't Going Your Way 167

Following a Poor Performance 169

Finished with High School Sports 171

OTHER..**174**

Committing to a College 175

Feeling Disconnected from God...................................177

Out with an Injury 179

Enduring Suffering..181

Contacted by a College 183

Winning the Fight Against Sin......................................185

Hurt by Christian Hypocrisy..187

Dealing with Shame 189

Preparing for the Future 191

The Week of State...193

Hopeless Against Sin..195

Doubting Your Salvation..197

During Spirit Week 199

Clarifying Your View of Eternity 201

Growing In the Fear of God 203

Your Plans Fell Apart..205

After Hearing a Sermon 207

Facing a Personal Problem..209

Life Seems Out of Control 211

Acknowledgments..214

About the Author 218

Notes..220

A WORD FROM AN OLYMPIAN

Ever since I was a little kid, I was fascinated by the concept of greatness. I looked up to great athletes such as Michael Jordan, great Christians such as Billy Graham, and great minds such as Albert Einstein. I was perplexed by the question: "Where does greatness come from?" At forty-two, I look back and see that my fascination with greatness was coming from the pure motive of wanting to be the "greatest" version of myself. As a kid, I wasn't sure what talents and abilities God had given me. All I knew was that I wanted to do the very best with my talents in the same way that those in the parable of the talents invested their talents and made them grow. I was burning (and am still burning) to do my best with whatever God had put inside me.

As I think about what I want most for you, the reader, it's that same exact thing. No one knows all the talents you've been given, and discovering those talents is going to be the best wild ride of your life. There is no telling what your true potential is whether it's in athletics, academics, or any other aspect of life. And you know what? The destination—how far you get with your talents—is really not what is important. What is important is being faithful with whatever talent you've been given and cultivating it to the very best of your ability. But how do you cultivate your talent? That's where *GAMEPLAN* comes in.

In *GAMEPLAN,* you will not only learn what it means and looks like to be a Christian who happens to be an athlete (not the other way around) but you will also have a toolbox you can pull out along your journey for those big and/or tricky moments that come up— when you need a manual to help you navigate the moment. Whether it's your first day of practice or you just faced a tough loss, you are going to need some wisdom and encouragement to help guide you through, which is exactly what *GAMEPLAN* is designed to do.

One realization I've had over the years as I've spent time strategizing about how I am going to develop talent and be "great" in the sense that I've used my God-given talent to the fullest is that, oftentimes, great people (such as David in the Old Testament) get tripped up in brief moments of weakness. It is so important, as we are on our own personal journeys, that we are aware of this common experience of great people throughout the ages. We must be prepared for those brief, yet really difficult times that will test us to our innermost being.

Where are we going to go for strength to get us through life's toughest moments? I like to think about my strategy as one that needs to be multifaceted. Meaning, you wouldn't go into battle with one arrow or bullet, would you? Of course not. You would want as much ammunition as possible for these moments. In the same way, when you find yourself in life's toughest moments, you want to know how to pray, worship, and seek wisdom and wise counsel from both trusted people and resources like *GAMEPLAN*.

I am very excited about this "arrow in your quiver" you are holding in your hands, and I pray it will give you strength when you need it the most and helpful guidance as you wade through deep water as a Christian. Many blessings to you on your journey!

– Ryan Hall, Olympian, author, coach, speaker

THE BIG QUESTION

Athlete, are you ready for a question that might change your life? Let's fast forward to your thirtieth birthday. In celebration of your big day, a group of your closest friends has come over for cake and games. While you're enjoying the birthday festivities, a knock on your door interrupts one of your party games. Noticing that all the guests have arrived, you're curious as to who it might be.

As you open the door, you are startled to be greeted by your favorite high school coach, who is holding a birthday present. You don't know how to respond. You haven't seen your coach since high school. Starting to feel awkward, you welcome your coach to the party and offer a piece of cake. Much to your surprise, your coach declines your invite and instead, kindly hands you a wrapped box, saying, "Here, I wanted to drop this by. Happy birthday."

No sooner is the gift in your hands than your former coach walks back to the car. Still a little baffled by the situation, you manage to choke out a brief "Thanks" before your former coach drives away. Turning from the door, you find all your friends with puzzled looks on their faces, wondering what happened.

"What's in the box?" one of them asks.

"I have no idea," you admit.

Without hesitation, you and your companions gather around as you carefully unwrap your coach's package. As more and more of the gift becomes visible, you begin to see what it is. Neatly framed in a plastic case is your old high school jersey. Although to your friends it looks like a worn-out piece of clothing, to you it represents a big part of your life.

"So what can you tell us about your high school sports career?" one of your friends asks.

Looking up from your jersey, you are met with a circle of blank stares, anticipating what you're going to say next . . .

Here's the big question: *When others ask about your high school sports career one day, what will you want your answer to be?*

Ultimately, the way you will answer that question depends on how you approach your sport right now. If you're like most athletes, the tragic reality is that one day you will look back on your high school sports career with little to talk about. Many high school athletes spend four years of their life competing in a way that loses much of its value the moment they graduate.

Thankfully, that doesn't have to be your story. God has a bigger and better desire for you. He wants you to approach sports not in the way the world does but with an entirely different approach—a kingdom approach.

That raises another great question: *What is a kingdom approach to sports?* Very simply, it is using sports to grow in your relationship with Jesus Christ while exalting Christ through sports. *GAMEPLAN* seeks to help you do both.

Within the pages of *GAMEPLAN* are 101 situational devotions, each marked with a specific situation when you would ideally read it. For example, there is a devotion to read at the start of a new season, one to read when you need inspiration, and even one for when you're struggling to trust God. Every devotion (except one) has been divided into one of five categories: preseason, practice, pre-competition, post-competition, and other. The purpose of dividing the devotions this way is to help you easily find the right devotion at the right time.

With that said, feel free to explore the devotions however you would like. *GAMEPLAN* has no schedule, no due date, and is not homework. It's a gameplan to help you take a kingdom approach to sports—and now it's in your hands. Are you ready to dive in? Check out the devotion titled "Read This First" to get started.

NOTE TO THE READER

Included within the pages of *GAMEPLAN* are numerous illustrations, some of which contain fictional, and others, factual information. Please note that those devotions referencing factual information include cited references.

READ THIS FIRST

When the Dodgers pinch hitter Kirk Gibson stepped up to the plate in Game 1 of the 1988 World Series, the stakes couldn't have been higher. It was the bottom of the ninth inning with one man on base, two outs, and the Dodgers were down by one. Gibson, who had two injured knees, prepared to square off against Oakland's Dennis Eckersley, who some would say at that time was the best relief pitcher in baseball.[1] (If you're getting lost in the baseball jargon, here's what you need to understand. Gibson was living nearly every kid's childhood dream. He was on the biggest stage, at the most crucial point of the game, with everything resting on his shoulders.)

Eckersley delivered the 3–2 pitch and Gibson connected, sending the ball over the right field wall for the walk-off win. Gibson limped around the bases and was mobbed by his teammates at home plate.[2]

Many consider Gibson's 1988 World Series game-winner to be the most clutch play in sports history. It's an incredible story that also happens to serve as a fitting introduction to what could be considered the most clutch play in human history. Here's how it went down.

Team humanity was in the hole. From the beginning of time, God created humankind to be in a personal relationship with Him. Tragically, every individual to ever live has fractured this relationship by choosing to live a life of disobedience toward God. Romans 3:23 puts it this way: "for all have sinned and fall short of the glory of God." To make matters worse, Romans 6:23 begins, "For the wages of sin is death." In other words, you and the rest of humanity were up against impossible odds. All had earned God's punishment by their wrongdoing and because of it had no way of restoring the relationship they were created for. Thankfully, the story doesn't end there.

Because of His love for the world, God sent His own Son, Jesus Christ, into the world. As a man, Jesus stepped up to the plate for humanity by living the life of perfect obedience that all people were supposed to live and dying the punishing death all people deserved to die. Romans 5:8 explains, "But God shows his love for us in that while we were still sinners, Christ died for us." As a result of His work, Jesus now offers the victory of a restored relationship with God to both you and all people. As the second half of Romans 6:23 explains, "The free gift of God is eternal life in Christ Jesus our Lord." Which brings us back to our story from the beginning.

When Gibson hit his game-winning home run, his teammates didn't remain in the dugout. They ran to meet him at home plate and join in the victory. In the same way, Jesus's death demands a response. Right now you have either surrendered to Jesus as your Savior or you are still in your sins. Living under Christ's lordship means receiving the saving work that Christ has accomplished on your behalf. Rejecting Christ's lordship is choosing to miss out on the only way to have a restored relationship with your Creator.

Are you ready to join in Christ's victory by running to Jesus and submitting to Him as Lord? Or are you content to sit defeated in the dugout?

APPLICATION:

If you're already a follower of Christ, that's tremendous. *GAME-PLAN* is for you! If not, it would be best for you to set this devotional aside and deal with that matter first. As a great starting place, read Romans 10:9–10 and Romans 10:13, which provide helpful guidance on how you can respond to the good news of Jesus's victory.

TIP:

Tomorrow is not guaranteed. If Jesus is not your Lord today, don't wait to surrender to Him.

PRESEASON

Starting a New Season 5

Remembering Your Identity 7

Getting a New Coach 9

After a Summer Weights Session..11

Talking Faith with Teammates 13

Ordering Sports Gear..15

During Summer Training Camp 17

Purifying Your Playlist 19

Kick-Starting Spiritual Growth...21

Saying No to Peer Pressure 23

Breaking Free from People Pleasing..25

Setting Season Goals 27

Finding a Role Model 29

Surrendering Social Media...31

Struggling to Trust God...33

Stressed Out 35

Beginning of the School Year..37

Using Your Time Wisely...39

Maximizing Your Gifts 41

Finding True Satisfaction 43

STARTING A NEW SEASON

The scene began in a typical fashion. It was June 6, 2023, and three Oklahoma Sooner softball players patiently sat in a press room answering reporters' questions. With Oklahoma preparing for their third consecutive national championship appearance, the pre-game press conference followed a rather routine script until ESPN reporter Alex Scarborough asked a probing question. "I know you talked about keeping the joy of the game, but I'm curious. It's a long season . . . and you guys have had the target on your back the entire time . . . How do you handle the unique pressure that comes with that [and] how do you keep the joy for so long?" That's when the conversation quickly moved from ordinary to extraordinary.

Shortstop Grace Lyons began, "Well, the only way that you can have a joy that doesn't fade away is from the Lord . . . there's no other way that softball can bring you that." Teammate Jayda Coleman continued, "I think that is what makes our team so strong is that we're not afraid to lose . . . because our life is in Christ." Finally, Alyssa Brito finished out the Sooner's trifecta: "Like they were saying, you can't find a fulfillment in an outcome whether it's good or bad . . . [We] play for something bigger and . . . that's just what brings . . . so much joy."[3][4]

Did you notice what all three of these college softball players had in common? They're satisfied; they're joyful. Grace, Jayda, and Alyssa were living the athletic dream of playing in the College World Series but had come to learn that true satisfaction and joy were found in something other than success. Although that mindset is largely uncommon in the world of sports, it is exactly what the Bible teaches.

In the book of Psalms, King David speaks on the topic of satisfaction and joy when He says of God in Psalm 16:11, "You make known to me the path of life; in your presence there is fullness of joy; at your right hand are pleasures forevermore." Fullness of joy. Pleasures forevermore. David is saying the way to find such blessings is to look to God. He further echoes this point as a command in Psalm 37:4, "Delight yourself in the LORD, and he will give you the desires of your heart."

Through these verses David is teaching us that having a relationship with God delivers a satisfaction and joy that are far greater than anything this world can offer, including winning. With this message fresh in our minds, we can now see more clearly how the words of Grace, Jayda, and Alyssa help expose an eye-opening reality. Winning a sport will never satisfy you at a soul level, and there's a reason for that—it was never meant to. As a human being, you were created to have a relationship with God. That relationship is the only thing that can bring you complete satisfaction and joy. Taking that truth to heart can have a profound impact on your life as an athlete because when you don't need winning to be satisfied, it makes winning that much sweeter.

APPLICATION:

Pick a time today to sit down and write a letter to your future self. This letter can be written the good old-fashioned way, with pen and paper, or through some electronic form. In the letter, encourage yourself with how your relationship with God satisfies you in ways that winning can't. Once you've finished, open a calendar and choose a date near the end of the season when you will read the letter. With your date selected, pick a safe location to store your letter until the time comes to open it up.

TIP:

Placing your letter in an obvious spot (or using a reminder system if written electronically) will keep you from forgetting to open the letter when your chosen date comes.

REMEMBERING YOUR IDENTITY

It was the start of a new week of practice, and the updated team schedule was freshly posted on the locker room door, outlining how every minute of practice would be spent. At first only a few athletes stood with curious faces looking at the paper, but before long, nearly the entire team was huddled around with puzzled looks. The schedule read:

- Film room: 3:00–3:30
- Conditioning: 3:30–3:45
- Drills and Mechanics: 3:45–4:15
- Team Plays: 4:15–4:45
- Warm-ups: 4:45–5:00

One of the athletes stated the obvious. "That doesn't make any sense. Why would warmups be at the end?"

You're probably thinking the same thing. Why would any coach ever put warmups at the end of practice? The whole point of warmups is to, well, warm up. The order makes all the difference. The same is true with two simple words: "Christian athlete." Order makes all the difference. We see this distinction come to life in Galatians 2:20 when Paul says, "I have been crucified with Christ. It is no longer I who live, but Christ who lives in me. And the life I now live in the flesh I live by faith in the Son of God, who loved me and gave himself for me."

Through these words Paul makes clear what defines him. Above all, Paul was a Christian; everything else in his life revolved around that fact.

Here's how this verse applies to you. The title "Christian athlete" is one that gets thrown around a lot; that's why it's essential to recognize which word comes first: *Christian*. You must remember that you're a Christian playing sports, not an athlete playing "Christian". Much like placing warmups at the end of a practice defeats the intended purpose of the activity, living in a way that prioritizes being an athlete before being a Christian defeats the intended purpose of competing.

APPLICATION:

It's time for you to create a focal point. To do this, simply pick an object that you will consistently see during practice and competition throughout the season. This can be a wristband, something you've written on your shoes, or even a scoreboard. The purpose of having this focal point will be to serve as a reminder of your true identity as a Christian.

TIP:

Focal points work best when you use them during a break in the action—moments like a drink break or a timeout.

GETTING A NEW COACH

Meet Michael Springs. During high school, Michael was a six -foot-three, 189-pound wrestler for Charles Herbert Flowers High School in Prince George's County, Maryland. Like many young athletes, Springs had a childhood filled with sports and the desire to outperform his older brother. Having both a combination of size and competitive background, at first glance, Springs checked all the boxes to be a potentially successful wrestler—except for one minor detail: he was blind. This left Springs with only one way to compete: trusting his coach.

During matches Springs would carefully listen to the voice of his coach, Odist Felder, who directed him against his opponent. Using phrases like "Stay in control" and "Circle left,"[5] Felder would instruct Springs as he battled on the mat. Together, this athlete-coach duo ultimately went on to qualify for state competition during Springs's second season of wrestling.

The story of Michael Springs and Odist Felder is an inspiring example of the power of trust between an athlete and a coach—a trust that resembles the relationship between a Christian and God. To get a better grasp on this relational trust, let's turn our attention to a passage that speaks of this topic.

Found within the wisdom-filled book of Proverbs is Proverbs 3:5–6, which instructs readers to "Trust in the LORD with all your heart, and do not lean on your own understanding. In all your ways acknowledge him, and he will make straight your paths." These verses provide believers not only with the command to trust God but also with the reason for trusting Him: He will lead you in the best way. Understanding this brings us back to the wrestling mat.

If we consider the story of Springs and Coach Felder, there's no question why they succeeded. The athlete-coach pair prospered because of their deep trust in one another. Similarly, the outcome of your life will be determined by the trust you place or don't place in God.

Proverbs 3:5–6 makes clear that God is willing to lead you. The question is, are you willing to trust Him?

APPLICATION:

Find time this week to ask your coach to go to lunch. While at lunch, do your best to get to know your coach better. You could ask questions like "Why did you start coaching?" and "How long have you been a coach?" Following your lunch, pick a book of the Bible to read that can help you know God better. As you go through the book, look specifically for lessons you can learn about God's character. When you come across these instances, write them down for future reference.

TIP:

Using a journaling Bible provides a helpful way to write down what you learn as you read God's Word.

AFTER A SUMMER WEIGHTS SESSION

Put yourself in the following situation: it's Monday morning, and you wake up to the sound of your obnoxious alarm. After feeling around for a bit, you finally find the source of your disturbance and palm it relentlessly until the noise stops. Peacefulness overcomes you as you sink back into your bed with your eyes closed. After what seems to be only a few moments, the irritating noise is back. This time as you feel around, getting ready to push the snooze button, you notice the time: 6:53 a.m. A rush of adrenaline shoots through your body, and you jump out of bed. You have seven minutes to make it to 7:00 a.m. weights, and it's a ten-minute drive to school. Frantically you throw on your clothes and rush out the door.

Twelve minutes later, you walk into the weight room and look at the clock: 7:05. You're late. *Great.* You quickly find your partner, who is setting up the squat rack.

"Hey, I was just getting the rack set up. Do you want to start warming up?"

You nod in agreement and step underneath the bar, resting the weight on your shoulders. "At least I made it for warm-ups," you mumble under your breath as you position your feet shoulder-width apart and slowly look up at the mirror in front of you. Suddenly a wave of disgust crosses your face, and you can hardly breathe. The shock of how you look is almost unbearable. You have pieces of food stuck in your teeth, your shirt has a large stain on the front, and your hair is a mess. In the morning's chaos you had completely forgotten to check how you looked. Right away you set down the bar. "I need to go to the bathroom," you say with embarrassment.

For many high schoolers, having an appearance that is less than ideal can be humiliating. Our illustration provides a great example of this, and it serves as an excellent foundation as we look at a passage of Scripture found in James 1:22–25: "But be doers of the word, and not hearers only, deceiving yourselves. For if anyone is a hearer of the word and not a doer, he is like a man who looks intently at his natural face in a mirror. For he looks at himself and goes away and at once forgets what he was like. But the one who looks into the perfect law, the law of liberty, and perseveres, being no hearer who forgets but a doer who acts, he will be blessed in his doing."

In these verses the Bible is likened to a mirror. James is saying that the Scriptures have the power to show believers both their own blemishes and what their perfect appearance should look like. However, looking into the mirror of God's Word is only half the equation.

Reading God's Word without responding would be similar to finding yourself in the embarrassing situation from before—late for weightlifting with a dreadful appearance—and then not doing anything about it. Both would be crazy. It's important to remember that your appearance is more than what you wear; it's the way you live too.

APPLICATION:

Applying what you read is an essential component of Bible study. The next time you read God's Word, put on your SPECS[6] by asking, Is there a . . .

1. S-in to forsake?
2. P-romise to claim?
3. E-xample to follow?
4. C-ommand to obey?
5. S-tumbling block to avoid?

TIP:

As you study God's Word, remember that your goal should be to learn *all* that the Bible teaches rather than ignoring the parts you don't want to hear.

TALKING FAITH WITH TEAMMATES

hree-hundred eighty-eight thousand, three-hundred seventy-five dollars. That was the price paid for a baseball sold at an auction in 2012. Why so much for a little white ball? The value came not from the ball itself but from who had signed it. Autographed by baseball legend Babe Ruth, the palm-sized sports relic became known as one of the most expensive Ruth signed balls in sports history.[7]

Nearly $400,000 is a lot of money for a ball with someone's name on it. Which begs the question, "Why does a signature have so much value?" Of course, the answer is surprisingly simple, and you probably could've guessed it. An autograph is a one-of-a-kind signature that no one else can replicate (at least legally).

How exactly this topic ties in with the Scriptures will become a little clearer after we look at two related passages. The first is Psalm 19:1, which says, "The heavens declare the glory of God, and the sky above proclaims his handiwork." The next comes from Romans 1:19–20: "For what can be known about God is plain to them, because God has shown it to them. For his invisible attributes, namely, his eternal power and divine nature, have been clearly perceived, ever since the creation of the world, in the things that have been made. So they are without excuse." Together, these two passages make the point that creation is God's autograph—His distinct, matchless, and personal trademark showing us He exists.

Much as a human autograph is exclusive to one person alone, creation is also unique to God alone—the only Being Who could ever create such a masterpiece. Unfortunately, every day countless people wake up in a world that they never take the time to look at and consider the beauty behind. If they did, it would only become clear that God exists, and creation is His autograph to prove it.

APPLICATION:

At this point you may be wondering how this devotion relates to talking faith with your teammates—that's where the application comes in. Often speaking to others about God can seem awkward and uncomfortable. You're unsure of what to say or how to say it. Now you don't have to be. Next time you find yourself in the middle of a good conversation, bring up the topic of "God's autograph" and share what you learned from this devotion. In the end you may be surprised at how valuable "God's autograph" can be when talking faith with your teammates.

TIP:

If one or more of your friends expresses interest in the topic of "God's autograph," share this devotion with them so they can read it themselves.

ORDERING SPORTS GEAR

Picture this. It's time for a new season to kick off, and you're ready to order a brand-new piece of sports gear. This year you've spent countless hours scanning the web before settling on the exact item you want. Not only do you have the item picked out, but you've also found it online at a huge discount. Although the website isn't a major retailer, you're reasonably confident it's a reliable source, so you type in your information and order the item. After waiting a few days, it finally arrives. As soon as the box hits your doorstep you're ripping into it, ready to try out your much-anticipated gear.

As you pull your gear out of the box, you hold it up with both hands and proudly display your prize. Carefully you flip the gear on all sides, enjoying the look and feel until you notice something. *That doesn't look quite right.* Immediately you begin to investigate the details of the gear a little more closely until your jaw drops, and you let out a loud shriek. "What? A counterfeit!" Upon careful inspection, you've discovered that the gear in the box was a knock-off version of what you've wanted all along. "This is absolutely unacceptable!" You set down the package in complete shock.

Hopefully this is not a situation you've ever encountered. Yet it provides a wonderful opportunity to explore the difference between a true believer and fake believer (a.k.a., counterfeit Christian)—a difference that can be clearly understood from Jesus's words in Matthew 15:8–9: "'This people honors me with their lips, but their heart is far from me; in vain do they worship me, teaching as doctrines the commandments of men.'"

The fundamental difference between a true and counterfeit Christian is found on the inside. Much like a counterfeit piece of gear, a counterfeit Christian can look very similar to the real deal but upon careful inspection proves to be fake. This inspection can be done by looking at the heart.

To help understand this, let's take for example two Christians. Both go to church twice a week, read their Bible an hour a day, and pray for thirty minutes before bed. From the outside they're the same. However, if you could see into their hearts, you would notice a difference. The first does those things so others will think they're a good person and because it makes them feel good about themselves, while the second does those things because they love God. Can you tell who's the counterfeit?

A person is not a Christian because he or she looks or acts a certain way. A Christian looks and acts a certain way because he or she loves God.

APPLICATION:

Take an honest look at your life and consider why you do the things you do. Are you looking for human praise and self-gratification or are you acting out of love for God? Although others may not be able to see your heart, God does.

TIP:

If you want to dive deeper into this topic, read Jesus's sermon found in Matthew chapters 5–7, where the Savior teaches the difference between outward religiosity and true love for God.

DURING SUMMER TRAINING CAMP

Gatorade. It's the pinnacle of sports drinks. Leading the industry with endorsements from top athletes and sponsorships from professional sports leagues, there's no question why Gatorade is the largest and most popular sports drink company in the United States.[8]

The iconic brand epitomizes sports drinks and undoubtedly has a substantial level of influence they put to use. The following words have been pulled directly from a Gatorade commercial used by the company as a promotional advertisement.

> *There's a moment . . . blink . . . you'll miss it. But in that second, the game changes everything. That first swing . . . step . . . look. The moment we ask, What if? What if we could go further, jump higher, or run the whole thing? What if we could be who we're meant to be? It can happen . . . if we're given the chance to play. And become who we look up to. That's when we find our stride. And tomorrow belongs to us. This is the moment it all starts. But only if we get the chance to have it . . . fuel tomorrow.[9]*

For many athletes, these are the types of words that send chills down their spines, inspiring them to strive for the greatest version of themselves. "What if we could be who we're meant to be?" The question has a thrilling ring to it, but before you can answer it, there's an even bigger question that needs to be answered first. Who are you meant to be?

The Bible does not leave that for you (or Gatorade) to decide. Romans 8:29 offers the answer: "For those whom he foreknew he also predestined to be conformed to the image of his Son, in order that he might be the firstborn among many brothers." The simple answer is, you are meant to be like Christ. Or in the words of Romans 8:29, "conformed to the image of his Son." How is this possible? Romans 6:4–5 explains: "We were buried therefore with him by baptism into death, in order that, just as Christ was raised from the dead by the glory of the Father, we too might walk in newness of life. For if we have been united with him in a death like his, we shall certainly be united with him in a resurrection like his." Jesus's work on the cross made it possible for you to be exactly who you were meant to be, exactly like Him.

Going back to the Gatorade commercial, we now have the one and only answer to their looming question. You can be who you were meant to be—and you were meant to be like Christ.

APPLICATION:

Grab your Bible and something to write on. Turn to the book of Ephesians and read through the first three chapters. Every time you read a description of who you are because of Christ, write it down. For example, Ephesians 1:3 says God has "blessed [you] in Christ with every spiritual blessing in the heavenly places." Mark down this description and keep the list going. When you reach the end of the three chapters, look back at everything you've written. That's who you are.

TIP:

Depending on how you count, you will be able to find twenty-five descriptions (including the one mentioned above) of who you are in Ephesians chapters 1–3. Tape this sheet of descriptions somewhere you'll be able to see them every day.

PURIFYING YOUR PLAYLIST

Athletes and music often go together in a package. If you attend any sporting event, you're likely to see countless athletes getting in the zone with music in their ears. As many athletes will tell you, it's not the lyrics they focus on but the beat. Although that perspective might sound harmless, as a Christian athlete, you are called to a higher standard. That's why we are going to take a personal dive into your workout playlist.

Don't worry; this won't take too long, but it will require active participation on your part. To begin, pull out your music listening device and open your workout playlist (if you don't have a workout playlist, select your favorite song). When your song is ready, give it a listen, and as you do, answer the following reflection questions:

- What lyrics are repeated in the song?
- What is the message of the song?
- What does this song motivate me to do?

Great job! With your song review complete, we can now turn our attention to a passage of Scripture that will provide us with a necessary standard to evaluate your song. We find that standard in Philippians 4:8: "Finally, brothers, whatever is true, whatever is honorable, whatever is just, whatever is pure, whatever is lovely, whatever is commendable, if there is any excellence, if there is anything worthy of praise, think about these things." In view of this passage, how did your song stand up? Was it great, or not so great? Regardless of the outcome, it's clear that Philippians 4:8 presents a high standard of thinking for a Christian—a standard that is practically impossible when you are filling your mind with corrupt lyrics.

Although the message here goes against the all-too-common excuse of blocking out the words and listening to the beat, it must be addressed. It is impossible to hear a song over and over without learning the lyrics. This topic can be a hard pill to swallow for many Christian athletes because listening to whatever you want is much easier than being selective with your music choices. But the One Who died for you desires that you honor Him in everything you do—including your music choices.

APPLICATION:

When you have some free time, make it a priority to run through the rest of your workout playlist (or list of favorite songs) and determine what songs need to go. As you evaluate, look for songs with corrupt content, sinful themes, or false worldviews. If you notice any songs labeled "explicit," it would be a good idea to eliminate those right away. As you go, you might find your playlist dwindling but don't lose heart. Over time you can find better songs that will fill your mind with what is true, honorable, just, pure, lovely, commendable, excellent, and worthy of praise.

TIP:

Simply because a song is labeled "Christian" or "secular" doesn't automatically make it good or bad. There are many other important things to consider, including the content of the lyrics and how they match up with the standard of Philippians 4:8.

KICK-STARTING
SPIRITUAL GROWTH

Take a quick look at your feet. If you're like most high school athletes, rocking the latest pair of kicks can be a big deal. In fact, athletes of all ages pride themselves on the shoes they lace up, putting a great deal of thought and effort into their daily footwear decisions—a passion that the leading shoe brands equally match. Every year shoe companies pay development teams top dollar to make the newest version of whatever's on your feet—featuring the latest designs, newest technology, and of course, the attractive names.

In his book *Kicksology* Brian Metzler expressed the continuous growth that defines the shoe market when he said, "Shoes are constantly evolving. And thanks to the continual ebb and flow of creative innovations, bizarre fads, and leaps in science and our understanding of the human body, they will continue to do so as long as humans are lacing up shoes."[10]

Although it may not seem like it at first glance, the way new shoes are produced yearly does have a correlation with your faith. The relationship between the two can be found in Ephesians 4:22–24, which says to, "Put off your old self, which belongs to your former manner of life and is corrupt through deceitful desires, and to be renewed in the spirit of your minds, and to put on the new self, created after the likeness of God in true righteousness and holiness."

The point is not that you should get a new pair of shoes to be more Christlike, but instead, that your faith should improve year after year just as shoes do. This truth is further exhibited in 2 Corinthians 4:16, which encourages believers: "So we do not lose heart. Though our outer self is wasting away, our inner self is being renewed day by day." The Christian life is intended to be a process of continuous growth in which we look more like Christ year after year.

To help us understand the importance of spiritual growth, let's try thinking about the topic from a slightly different angle. How excited would you be if shoe companies came out with the same pair of shoes every year? The same look, same feel, same performance, same everything. Odds are you wouldn't be overly thrilled. If that's how you would feel about a pair of shoes, then it's reasonable to suggest that God wouldn't be thrilled to see you look the exact same every year either, and neither should you. God wants you to look more like Christ, and that requires growth.

The good news is that God has already provided you with four primary avenues for spiritual growth: Bible study, prayer, regular fellowship with other believers, and hearing God's Word preached (church can provide a great place to do the last two). As you put these into practice, you grow spiritually.

APPLICATION:

Which of the four spiritual avenues mentioned in the lesson (Bible study, prayer, fellowship with Christians, listening to preaching) could use the most attention in your life? Choose one of the four areas to start making changes in right away. Although the changes will likely be different for you than anyone else, the goal is the same—to look more like Christ.

TIP:

Keep in mind that although you have a responsibility to continually become more like Christ, your spiritual growth is ultimately a work of God. Remembering this can help prevent you from developing the unhealthy mindset of "never doing enough."

SAYING NO TO PEER PRESSURE

"These are the special-edition, all-white retros that I was telling you about," Jessica proudly stated. The sophomore carefully lifted up her brand-new pair of shoes for her entire circle of friends to admire. After receiving a few compliments, Jessica slowly dropped the shoes to the ground and slid her feet into her prized possession. Tenderly she tied the laces and stood tall with a delightful smile on her face. That is until she noticed the path her friends were taking in front of her. Directly opposite Jessica was a small mud puddle no deeper than a half-inch but deadly in Jessica's mind. *There's absolutely no way.* She shook her head. *No, I can't walk through that with my white shoes.* Having settled the matter, Jessica turned around and walked a different way.

Have you ever met someone who had recently bought a brand-new pair of entirely white shoes? If you have, there are typically two things you'll notice. Number one, the shoes. Number two, the extended effort of that person to keep his or her shoes white. Interestingly enough, this does have a spiritual parallel.

In James 1:27 believers are taught that "Religion that is pure and undefiled before God the Father is this: to visit orphans and widows in their affliction, and to keep oneself unstained from the world." A similar point is made in Proverbs 25:26: "Like a muddied spring or a polluted fountain is a righteous man who gives way before the wicked." Notice the overlap between these two verses. In both instances Godly living is described in terms of purity and giving way to the things of the world as bringing defilement. This is where white shoes tie in.

As a believer, God calls you to purity in your everyday life. Unfortunately, you live in a world filled with people who don't have that same mission. Much like the situation encountered by Jessica, you will often find yourself in positions in which you will have to decide. Will you walk in the way of the world and join in with defilement it brings, or will you choose a different path for the sake of purity? Although you might be mocked for trying to be pure in what you watch, how you act, and the things you wear, that's nothing to be ashamed of. God will be pleased, and you will stay pure.

APPLICATION:

Refusing to join in when your friends are doing wrong can be hard, but having a plan in place for what you will do instead can help. Consider when you are most tempted to give in to peer pressure. For each situation that comes to mind, create a plan of action for how you will respond next time. Although each situation you encounter may be unique, having a general idea of how you will respond will save you from trying to come up with something at the moment. For example, if you find yourself in a conversation that turns bad, use it as an opportunity to take a bathroom break.

TIP:

Want some more encouragement about how to respond to peer pressure? Check out Hebrews 2:18—Jesus can relate and He's ready to help.

BREAKING FREE FROM PEOPLE-PLEASING

It's draft day. For many fans, that means sitting back and watching their favorite professional sports team pick top college players to join the roster. This is often an enjoyable experience for most devotees who have the privilege of watching the future of their team unfold. However, it is a different story for those behind the scenes making the picks. Former NFL general manager, Thomas Dimitroff, describes the reality of the job:

> There was a lot of pressure on me, and no one (other than team owner Arthur Blank) made it more apparent than the highly regarded sportswriter Peter King, who came over to my house during the predraft process that year. While talking . . . he said something along the lines of, "You know, Thomas, if you screw this [2008 NFL Draft] up . . . you and your family will no longer be living in this beautiful house in Buckhead, but instead may be living back in Boulder in your humble three-bedroom home . . ." We laughed, of course. But . . . I was taken aback about how upfront and real Peter was about the situation. And it was true: I was hanging on for dear life.[11]

The eye-opening words of Dimitroff make one thing alarmingly clear. The pick a general manager makes on draft day will ultimately change his or her life. Ironically, this is a reality that relates to your own life more than you probably realize.

Comparable to draft day in the world of sports is a type of draft day in your life as a believer, though you likely don't call it that. Paul refers to this type of personal draft day in Galatians 1:10 when he writes, "For am I now seeking the approval of man, or of God? Or am I trying to please man? If I were still trying to please man, I would not be a servant of Christ."

Paul's words make one thing clear: you will inevitably make an important pick in your life, and that's who you are going to please. You can pick God, yourself, friends, parents, or someone on social media you don't even know. But much like Dimitroff's decision, whoever you choose will change your life. If you want to live a fulfilling, content, and satisfying life, then your pick must be God. There are no other options. That's who Paul picked. Who are you going to choose?

APPLICATION:

The idea of a Christian draft day may come off as an oversimplification, but in all practicality, a wrong pick can result in some pretty complicated mistakes. Try choosing which of the erroring characters below you most often relate to:

- Divided Dan: Tries to please more than one person at a time; an impossible task.

- Flippy Francis: Often switches between who he's trying to please; a tiring pursuit.

- Erring Erica: Has decided to please herself; a fatal mistake.

Each of these characters represents a potential problem that can arise in the life of a believer, and each can be easily avoided by deciding to make God your exclusive pick.

TIP:

Keep in mind that valuing the opinions of family, friends, and those in authority is different than people pleasing.

SETTING SEASON GOALS

Nearly every athlete at some point in his or her career has dreamed of making it to the top, whether that means being a world champion, record-holder, or achieving some other distinguishing mark. This desire often springs from a dream of a promised glory, fame, and prestige that supposedly comes with being on top. It's an enticing thought, but before you or anyone else dedicates countless hours trying to make it there (wherever "the top" is for you), it might be wise to hear from someone who already has.

In his book *From the Outside: My Journey through Life and the Game I Love*, former professional basketball star Ray Allen shared what it's like from the top when he wrote about the days after winning an NBA championship. "And yet, as the days wore on, there was a part of me that felt empty . . . It had more to do with having always believed that when you win a championship, you're transported to some new, exalted place. What I realized was that you are the same person you were before, and that if you are not content with who you are, a championship, or any accomplishment, isn't going to change that."[12]

The reality that Allen exposed in his book isn't new. Long before Allen experienced the emptiness of the world's promises himself, Solomon, ancient Israel's wealthiest and wisest king, revealed the same truth. In Ecclesiastes 2:8–10 we read, "I also gathered for myself silver and gold and the treasure of kings and provinces. I got singers, both men and women, and many concubines, the delight of the sons of man. So I became great and surpassed all who were before me in Jerusalem. Also my wisdom remained with me. And whatever my eyes desired I did not keep from them. I kept my heart from no pleasure, for my heart found pleasure in all my toil, and this was my reward for all my toil."

In essence, King Solomon is saying he got everything he ever wanted. He made it to the tippy top. And what did he find there? Verse 11 give us the answer. "Then I considered all that my hands had done and the toil I had expended in doing it, and behold, all was vanity and a striving after wind, and there was nothing to be gained under the sun." What's at the top? Absolutely nothing.

The words of both Allen and King Solomon serve as a warning. Don't spend your time and energy expecting to find something at the top that isn't there. The world might be full of promises about the glory of being the best, but they aren't true. In your own life it might be your desire to win a state title or be the best on your team. But if you're looking for meaning in your sport, don't look to the top. Look to Christ. That's the only place you'll find true fulfillment.

APPLICATION:

As you set goals for the season ahead, try directing your attention away from performance goals in favor of setting heart goals. As the name implies, a heart goal focuses on what's happening inside you rather than outside. An example of a heart goal would be to compete with a heart of courage. Like many goals, achieving these marks will require dependency on God and discipline as you cultivate your chosen attribute(s) throughout the season.

TIP:

Heart goals offer a healthy alternative to performance goals, which often depend on factors outside your control.

FINDING A ROLE MODEL

Early in the 2013–2014 NBA season the San Antonio Spurs were facing the Cleveland Cavaliers.[13] Shortly into the first quarter, what seemed like an ordinary play turned into a masterpiece as the Spurs exemplified what true teamwork looks like.

Point guard Patty Mills began the possession by passing the ball to number 21, Tim Duncan. After making his pass, Mills quickly made a double cut to the basket and filled a gap outside in the corner. Not seeing an opening, Duncan pump-faked toward Mills and waited as power forward Matt Bonner set a down screen for number 20, Manu Ginóbili. Breaking free from his defender, Ginóbili received a pass from Duncan, who followed with a ball screen. Using Duncan's screen, Ginóbili drove to the basket and kicked the ball out to Mills. Taking the pass, Mills quickly relayed the ball to Danny Green, who nailed an open three-pointer near the top of the key.[14]

If you got lost trying to follow all the details of that play, it's okay. All you need to know is that it summarizes the unforgettable season of teamwork the Spurs displayed as they worked together to become the 2013–2014 NBA Champions.[15] Their style of play that year would go on to be described during a late-season game when an NBA broadcaster commented, "Everyone's got a spot—they fill it."[16]

That simple description should ring true not only for the 2013–2014 Spurs but also for every follower of Christ. We see this idea come to life in Ephesians 4:15–16: "Rather, speaking the truth in love, we are to grow up in every way into him who is the head, into Christ, from whom the whole body, joined and held together by every joint with which it is equipped, when each part is working properly, makes the body grow so that it builds itself up in love." Packed within these two verses is God's incredible design for Christian teamwork. They describe the reality that all true Christians are on a team created to work together. This draws us back to our play from the beginning.

If you were to take any one of the five San Antonio players out of the picture, it wouldn't work. Every player had a spot to fill. In the same way, God has specifically designed you and every other follower of Christ to play a unique role on His team. When each member of God's team fills his or her spot and works together, it forms a beautiful masterpiece that brings God glory and works for everyone's growth.

APPLICATION:

Think of one godly Christian in your life whom you look up to. This may be a believer at your church, school, or even a relative. Reach out to that person and see if he or she would be willing to disciple you. If the person is willing, make it a priority to find a good time/day in his or her schedule to meet with you regularly.

TIP:

If the idea of pursuing a discipleship relationship makes you nervous, keep in mind that the aim of discipleship is simply for one Christian, usually older in the faith, to help another Christian follow Christ.

SURRENDERING SOCIAL MEDIA

"Are you kidding me?" Sarah raged. The high school sophomore could barely hold herself together. On cue with her outburst, the entire table of high school girls looked up from their phones to see what the problem was. "What is this?" she continued. "I just changed my password."

"What's wrong?" one of her friends asked.

Sarah snapped her head up from her phone screen and stared directly at her friend. "Look at this!" She shoved her phone in front of her friend. Smack-dab in the middle of Sarah's phone screen were the words "Sorry, your password was incorrect." Tears began to well up in Sarah's eyes. "I'm . . . *sniff* . . . locked out of my account. *Sniff sniff.*"

There is a lot that could be said about social media . . . a lot. So, with there being so many important things for a Christian athlete to know, where's a good place to start? As with anything, the best place to start is the Word of God, which is exactly where we will begin. The verse of choice might be one you wouldn't expect for this topic. It's found in Romans 10:9, which says, "Because, if you confess with your mouth that Jesus is Lord and believe in your heart that God raised him from the dead, you will be saved."

While Romans 10:9 is a verse about salvation, it also has a signifi-cant overlap with social media. Here's the logic:

1. If you are a Christian, that means Jesus is your Lord.

2. If Jesus is your Lord, that means He rules over all your life.

3. If Jesus rules over all your life, that means Jesus is Lord over your social media accounts.

Here's the difficulty. It's much easier to give God partial access to your accounts or lock Him out altogether than to let Him use your social media for His glory.

31

Although there are many things that a Christian athlete needs to think about when it comes to using social media in a God-glorifying way, those things will fall in line only after you recognize God as the Lord of your social media accounts.

You might think being locked out of your social media account is bad. But it's even worse if God is locked out. Does God have your passwords?

APPLICATION:

If God were in charge of your social media account, would it look the way it does now? Here are a few steps to help make any necessary changes:

1. Open your social media account(s) home screen and review your posts. Do you notice any unfitting images or descriptions for a follower of Christ? Go ahead and press the "delete" button on those.

2. Return to your home screen and tap "following." Scroll through the list of those you follow, and unfollow any accounts that cause you to sin.

3. Finally, make your way to the account search page to look for Christian accounts that share faithful, biblical content with their followers that you can begin following.

TIP:

Many phones offer the ability to set a daily "time limit" on how much time you can spend using any given app. If you tend to spend more time on social media than you should, start setting time limits on your social media apps.

STRUGGLING TO TRUST GOD

"There's no way!" blurted the sophomore as he closed his locker. Before he could continue, his best friend objected, "Yes, way! It seriously happened."

The conversation continued as the two friends walked down the hallway.

"You're telling me that you threw a basketball from the top of the bleachers into the basketball hoop on the playground. Impossible. That's at least fifty feet, and there's like four trees in the way."

Rather than continue the bantering, the friend boasting of the trick shot opened his eyes wide and gave a few exaggerated head nods.

His skeptical friend continued. "That's something I'm going to have to see to believe."

The moral of this story is not about honesty, and it's not about fighting; it's about trust—a very important topic when it comes to your relationship with God. As we'll see from the story below, God can be trusted.

In the thirteenth century BC,[17] God's chosen people, the nation of Israel, were being held captive as slaves in Egypt. Through an incredible display of events, God saved the Israelites from their captors and led them by the hand of His chosen leader, Moses, into the wilderness. As they journeyed through the desert, the Israelites began to complain to Moses that they didn't have meat to eat; Moses wasn't having it. He took the issue to God and made clear that he wasn't happy about having all of God's children complaining to him with their problems. God responded to Moses with a simple solution; He would feed the nation. Moses's reaction to God's plan is found in Numbers 11:21–22: "But Moses said, 'The people among whom I am number six hundred thousand on foot, and you have said, "I will give them meat, that they may eat a whole month!" Shall flocks and herds be slaughtered for them and be enough for them? Or shall all the fish of the sea be gathered together for them, and be enough for them?'"

Moses's response is clear; he lacked trust in God's ability to do what He said. God's reply to Moses's doubts comes later in the chapter, in Numbers 11:23, 31: "And the LORD said to Moses, 'Is the LORD's hand shortened? Now you shall see whether my word will come true for you or not.'... Then a wind from the LORD sprang up, and it brought quail from the sea and let them fall beside the camp, about a day's journey on this side and a day's journey on the other side."

Similar to the skeptical sophomore's doubt of his friend's claims, we can often find ourselves in situations when trusting God's Word can prove challenging. When these temptations spring up in your life, it's important to remind yourself that God is the most powerful, wise, and loving Being of all time, and He has your best interests at heart. If He cared enough to send His Son for you, you can be confident that He cares enough to do what's best for you.

APPLICATION:

When it comes to trusting God, it's helpful to remember there's a difference between feeling and acting. Although you may not feel like trusting God in every moment, it is your responsibility to act in a way that demonstrates your trust in Him. In what ways can you show God that you trust Him in the situation you are currently encountering?

TIP:

Depending on your situation, trust can sometimes mean performing some action, and at other times it can mean waiting. If you're struggling to know which to do, pray about it and ask a few older Christians for their wisdom.

STRESSED OUT

It was the final game of the 1998 NBA Championship and ten seconds remained on the clock. The Chicago Bulls were down by one, and everyone's eyes rested on one player: Michael Jordan. Time slowly ticked away as Jordan sized up the defense and then made his move. With a quick drive to the lane and step-back crossover, the NBA All-Star freed himself in time to release the ball . . . swish.[18] That shot clinched the championship for the Bulls and marked MJ's twenty-eighth game-winner.[19]

Throughout his career Jordan proved to be the go-to player when a game came down to the wire. If time was running out, teams would rest their confidence in the hands of the all-time great. In doing so, they demonstrated a faith in MJ that should challenge us to remember the type of faith Christians are to have in God. Unfortunately, this faith in God does not always come easy.

Often life can throw at us circumstances that cause us to feel that our hands are full. These stresses of life have been an ever-present reality throughout all of history. Thankfully, Peter, a disciple of Jesus, offered direction for handling stress when he urged believers in 1 Peter 5:6–7, "Humble yourselves, therefore, under the mighty hand of God so that at the proper time he may exalt you, casting all your anxieties on him, because he cares for you." Pay special attention to the end of that passage because it teaches an important point.

No matter your situation or the stress it's causing you, you can cast it on God because He genuinely cares about you. God is not merely watching your situation from afar, hoping you figure it out. He's waiting for you to give Him whatever is stressing you out. Or, put another way, pass Him the ball. Thinking in those terms brings us back to where we started.

Throughout your life you will inevitably encounter situations that feel like the 1998 NBA championship. You may feel as if you're down by one, time is running out, and the ball is in your hands. When you find yourself in those moments, follow the example of the Chicago Bulls and pass the ball to someone Who can be trusted. When you rest your confidence in the hands of God, as the Bulls did MJ, and leave the final outcome of your situation up to Him, He will never let you down.

APPLICATION:

It's time to let go of the stress you've been holding onto and "pass" it to God. Take a moment to release to God whatever you're struggling with by praying about your stress. As you pray, it might help to put your hands into a fist and then physically release them. When you release control of your stress, your hands are open to take hold of the peace God freely offers.

TIP:

As you cast your burden on the Lord, consider the comforting promise of Philippians 4:6–7: "Do not be anxious about anything, but in everything by prayer and supplication with thanksgiving let your requests be made known to God. And the peace of God, which surpasses all understanding, will guard your hearts and your minds in Christ Jesus."

BEGINNING OF THE SCHOOL YEAR

Congratulations! You have been selected to represent your high school sports team in an initiative to get local youth active. The location of your speech will be at a nearby elementary school where you will get the opportunity to speak to a first-grade class about your sport. It has been requested that you simplify your sport down to one or two sentences that the first-graders can understand. For example, a tennis player might say, "Tennis is a sport in which two people hit a ball back and forth over a net. You win by either getting the ball past the other player or when that player is unable to return the ball." Are you ready? It's your turn. Take a moment to develop a definition for your sport that would be ready for the first-graders. (Don't worry this devotion will wait for you until you're done.)

Great! With your definition complete, let's turn our attention to a passage of Scripture found in Jeremiah 10:3–5 that will help us connect your definition with the Word of God. In this passage the prophet says, "For the customs of the peoples are vanity. A tree from the forest is cut down and worked with an axe by the hands of a craftsman. They decorate it with silver and gold; they fasten it with a hammer and nails so that it cannot move. Their idols are like scarecrows in a cucumber field, and they cannot speak; they have to be carried, for they cannot walk. Do not be afraid of them, for they cannot do evil, neither is it in them to do good."

In our culture, sports are often elevated to the level of an idol. Unfortunately, idolizing something as simple as your sport doesn't make sense. In these verses Jeremiah pointed out the nonsense behind the idol worship of his day. Although the idols of Jeremiah's time looked much different than they do now the message of this passage is still appropriate.

Think back to the definition you gave your sport. Consider how ridiculous it would be to let something so simple interfere with your relationship with God! When you elevate your sport to a level that gets in the way of your relationship with God, it sadly becomes an idol. Go ahead and play your sport. Enjoy your sport. But never let your sport be your god.

APPLICATION:

Children love looking up to athletes, especially athletes they can watch in person. Choose a local elementary school in your area to contact, asking if you would be able to talk with one of their elementary classes about your sport. (If your high school is already connected with an elementary, that will only make things easier.) During your presentation, make sure to include how your faith shapes the way you approach your sport.

TIP:

If public speaking is not your thing, don't worry. Most elementary students won't care about your presentation skills.

USING YOUR TIME WISELY

In cycling they call it the hour record. The rules are simple: "Ride as fast as you can around a velodrome for one hour. Go further [*sic*] than anyone else has before, and the hour record is yours."[20] To an average person it sounds like torture. For the world of cycling it's one of the greatest accomplishments possible. With the hour record being repeatedly rebroken since its origin in 1876, the task comes with a particularly intimidating thought: every second counts.

Strangely enough, that simple thought is quite biblical. To understand how, we need to start by reframing our understanding of time in general.

First, it's necessary to recognize that time is a gift from God. James 1:17 says, "Every good gift and every perfect gift is from above, coming down from the Father of lights, with whom there is no variation or shadow due to change." Do you know what's included in "every good gift and every perfect gift"? Time. Every moment of your life is a gift from God, including this moment right now. That's why Ephesians 5:15–16 offers the command: "Look carefully then how you walk, not as unwise but as wise, making the best use of the time, because the days are evil." Not only is time a gift from God, but it's also to be used wisely.

In the context of the hour record there's no doubt that time is of the essence. However, the same could be said about your life on earth. God has gifted you with twenty-four hours every day. You can use it or waste it, but you will never get it back. The question is, how are you spending your time?

APPLICATION:

Pick a day this week to track how you spend your time. As you go throughout the day, keep a running list (physical or digital) of what you did and how long you spent doing it. Your list may look something like this:

- Breakfast: 7:00–7:20
- School prep: 7:20–7:35
- Instagram: 7:35–7:50
- Drive to school: 7:50–7:55
- And so on . . .

Once you've reached the end of the day, go back through your list and review how you spent your time. What activities were the most time-consuming? Were there any areas in which you spent more time than you realized? Remember: God calls you as a Christian to make the "best use of the time." Use this activity as a way to recognize the areas in which you can better spend the time you've been given.

TIP:

Instead of writing down every activity the moment you finish, simply make a note of the start time and end time alongside a key word to help remember what you did. Then you can come back later to fill in the details.

MAXIMIZING YOUR GIFTS

You only have to take one look at the highly recognized Christian athlete Tim Tebow to see that God has gifted him in an abundance of ways. Take for example Tebow's athletic talent, which he used to claim two college football national championships and contracts as a professional football and professional baseball player.[21] Or consider Tebow's spiritual gifting, which has led him to establish the highly charitable Tim Tebow Foundation, boldly share his Christian faith on primetime ESPN, and cause the Bible verse John 3:16 to go viral on multiple occasions.[22] [23] You could even take into account Tebow's creative skill, which he has utilized to write multiple *New York Times* best-selling Christian books and produce a box-office, top-ten Christian movie.[24] [25]

When it comes to the topic of gifting, Tim Tebow is clearly a fitting subject. However, what makes Tebow of particular importance to us is not only his gifts but also how he has used those gifts—a matter of true significance throughout the teachings of Christ.

In Matthew 25 Jesus taught His disciples a parable commonly called The Parable of the Talents. In Jesus's story a master was going away on a journey and divided up his wealth among three servants. Each servant was given a different amount of money, and each was responsible for how he would use that wealth. Two servants used their master's money wisely and gained even more wealth, while the third servant hid his master's money out of fear of failing. When the master finally returned, he was well pleased with the first two servants, saying to each in verses 21 and 23, "Well done, good and faithful servant. You have been faithful over a little; I will set you over much. Enter into the joy of your master." His response toward the third servant in verse 26 was much less favorable, saying, "You wicked and slothful servant!" and then casting him away.

Although Jesus's words were spoken centuries ago, the lesson this parable teaches still applies to believers today. Jesus is the manager who has departed for heaven and given every believer different gifts. His desire is for His followers to use those gifts until He returns, at which point He will reward them for their labor. The moral of the story is not about how much you have been given but how you use it. Understanding this leads us to a surprising conclusion.

Much as with the servants in The Parable of the Talents, Jesus's expectation from you is the exact same as it is from someone like Tim Tebow—that expectation is faithfulness. Whether your gifting looks like writing best-selling books or encouraging notes to your teammates, Jesus's ultimate concern is how you use what He has given you. Your gifts may look different than others, but they are no less important in Jesus's sight. One day you will give an account for how you have used your gifts, and on that day you will want to hear the words "Well done, good and faithful servant."

APPLICATION:

The first step to using your gifts is recognizing what they are. Take a few moments to sit down and write a list of the circumstances, opportunities, and talents (both spiritual and physical) that God has given you. As you do, you may find it helpful to ask other Christians in your life how they think you may be gifted. Once you've completed your list, prayerfully consider how you might best use your God-given gifts to make an impact for God's kingdom.

TIP:

Check out the following two passages that list the different spiritual gifts given to Christians: Romans 12:6-8 and 1 Corinthians 12:4-11, 28.

FINDING TRUE SATISFACTION

If you were to rank the greatest football players of all time, quarterback Tom Brady would inevitably be in the discussion. With a long list of jaw-dropping accomplishments, including records for the most Super Bowl championships, regular-season wins, and touchdown passes,[26] it's easy to see why many consider Brady one of the greatest quarterbacks to ever live.

In light of his great success, it should be no surprise that his book, *The TB12 Method*, became a #1 *New York Times* bestseller shortly after its release.[27] In the book, Brady describes the key training methods he credits for helping him improve year after year.[28] Of those key methods, Brady puts a special emphasis on nutrition, which he devotes an entire chapter of the book to. Here's how he starts the chapter: "If you don't pay attention to what you put inside your body, or if you ignore the connection between good nutrition and healthy muscles, then you're not giving yourself the opportunity to achieve your peak performance."[29]

Odds are you already knew nutrition was important before you read that; however, hearing it from one of the greatest football players to ever live might make you think twice about what you feed your body. If that's the case with Brady, how much more should the words of Jesus, the greatest person to ever live, deserve our fullest attention? When Jesus was on earth, He spoke about a different type of nutrition on multiple occasions—what you feed your soul. Let's take a moment to dive into one of these instances.

Jesus was coming off the miraculous feeding of more than 5,000 people. As might be expected, the crowd followed Jesus as He moved to a new location with His disciples. Seeing the great multitudes pursuing Him, Jesus used the opportunity to instruct the masses. In John 6:27 Jesus said, "Do not work for the food that perishes, but for the food that endures to eternal life, which the Son of Man will give to you."

Confused, the crowd began questioning what Jesus meant by this rather odd statement. Jesus replied a few verses later in John 6:35 with these words: "I am the bread of life; whoever comes to me shall not hunger, and whoever believes in me shall never thirst." At first glance this verse may appear rather puzzling. However, the intended message is actually quite simple.

Much like our bodies have physical needs, our souls have spiritual needs. Brady made clear the importance of what you feed your body, and through these passages Jesus made clear the importance of what you feed your soul. Practically speaking, you feed your soul with the things you look at, listen to, and think about, all of which impact you at a heart level. Unfortunately, many people choose to feed their souls with the scraps this world has to offer rather than looking to Jesus—the only One Who can truly satisfy.

APPLICATION:

Do a quick rundown of your day and consider the different ways you look for satisfaction. What do you read, watch, listen to, and think about? Narrow your search to a few items you know you shouldn't feed your soul but still choose to. Once you've settled on a few areas, ask yourself the following question for each: "How is Christ more satisfying than [blank]?" or "What am I trying to get from [blank] that I should look for Christ to provide?"

TIP:

Many phones have a screen time feature that will allow you to see how you spend your time on the device. If you have that option, give yours a look and see if it reveals any areas of concern.

PRACTICE

First Practice 47

Learning the Playbook 49

Start of a New Week 51

Hard Day at Practice 53

After a Morning Practice................................55

Mid-Season Boredom 57

Making Sacrifices..59

Facing the Fear of Others 61

Feeling Discouraged 63

Going Through a Trial......................................65

Convicted Over Sin 67

Standing Up Against Bullying.........................69

Frustrated with a Teammate..........................71

Burdened Beyond Bearing 73

Missed a Practice 75

Feeling Stuck In Your Routine 77

Getting Home from Practice 79

Serving Your Teammates 81

Watching Your Words.....................................83

Sharing the Gospel 85

Needing Inspiration..87

Resisting Temptation 89

Following a Film Session.................................91

Unhappy with Your Circumstances.................93

Staying on Your Guard....................................95

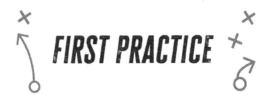

FIRST PRACTICE

When Hall of Fame football coach Vince Lombardi walked into the Green Bay Packers training camp during the summer of 1961, he didn't start by sharing a long list of goals, an incredible motivational speech, or even his plans for that year. No, Coach Lombardi started somewhere much simpler. With a football in his hand and thirty-eight professional football players listening, Coach Lombardi made a profound statement: "Gentlemen, this is a football."[30] The legendary coach began at square one with his players, and his emphasis on the basics didn't stop there.

Throughout the remainder of the training camp, Lombardi's focus continued to remain on the fundamentals. As he reviewed with his players how to block and tackle, the drills could have easily been considered elementary for a professional football team. But for Coach Lombardi, who never had a losing season in his entire career as a professional head football coach, it worked year after year.

Coach Lombardi is not alone when it comes to stressing the importance of the basics. In fact, the same principle can be found throughout the Scriptures. Let's take a look at one such example that points out this mindset. It's found in 1 Corinthians 3:1–2 where Paul relayed a very simplistic message to the Corinthian church: "But I, brothers, could not address you as spiritual people, but as people of the flesh, as infants in Christ. I fed you with milk, not solid food, for you were not ready for it. And even now you are not yet ready."

In other words, Paul was telling the Corinthian church that they weren't growing in their relationship with Christ. Why? Because they had neglected the fundamentals of the faith. What exactly are the fundamentals? They are the means God has provided for your growth as a Christian—things like Bible reading, prayer, and involvement in a local church.

Although those fundamentals might not come off as flashy or exciting, they are incredibly important. Coach Lombardi's success on the football field proved this in the world of sports, and you can be confident that the fundamentals of your faith will prove to be even more important in your Christian walk.

APPLICATION:

Find a time this week to sit down and outline what your daily schedule will look like this sports season. This may include class schedule, practice time, school commitments, and so on. Once you've completed your outline, evaluate which points throughout the day/week it would be ideal for you to spend time in God's Word, in prayer, and at church.

TIP:

If you're waiting for your schedule to free up before spending time with God, you will never end up getting to it. The fundamentals of the faith must come as a first priority in your life, not as an afterthought.

LEARNING THE PLAYBOOK

Smack!

The large stack of papers landed flatly on the table. It was the first day of girls' lacrosse practice and the coach was handing out playbooks.

Smack! Smack! Smack!

The sound continued until every girl had a freshly printed playbook directly in front of her. As each player began to flip through her own stack of pages, it became obvious who the freshmen were by their wide eyes and pale faces.

It wasn't long before one of the young players had the guts to speak up. "Um, Coach . . ." stumbled the freshman as she flipped through the large stack of papers. "Are we supposed to learn . . . all of this?"

"You bet," the coach said enthusiastically. "That's why I gave you your very own."

After a short silence, one of the senior girls offered encouragement. "Don't worry . . . it seems like a lot, but take it one day at a time. You can learn it."

This story relates a common perspective that many Christians can have toward the Bible. They see the Bible as the freshmen girls saw the playbook—an enormously large book with so much to read and countless things to learn. Unfortunately, that can be the reason that God's playbook, the Bible, sometimes sits unopened on the shelves of many believers, collecting dust.

Thankfully, the Bible itself offers some encouragement.

In 2 Timothy 3:16–17 we find these words: "All Scripture is breathed out by God and profitable for teaching, for reproof, for correction, and for training in righteousness, that the man of God may be complete, equipped for every good work." Theses verses are an excellent reminder of why you need the Bible. God's Word promises to provide you with exactly what you need for the Christian life. You could say that it equips you with the "plays" for life.

Yes, like most other playbooks, the Bible can be overwhelming at first, stretching your brain at times, and often challenges you, but don't let that discourage you. With dedication and commitment, you can learn God's Word—one day at a time.

APPLICATION:

Find time this evening to go online and search for a Bible-reading plan that grabs your attention. You might try searching "Chronological Bible Reading Plan," "Old/New Testament Bible Reading Plan," or "One-Year Bible Reading Plan." Once you find a plan that interests you, save and/or print the plan and track your progress as you complete each day's reading.

TIP:

Many Bibles have reading plans included in the back pages, or if you prefer reading digitally, you can often find Bible apps with free built-in reading plans.

START OF A NEW WEEK

Tick, tick . . . bzzz, rattle, rattle, woosh. Crack [silence]. Tick, tick . . . bzzz, rattle, rattle, woosh. Crack [silence]. Tick, tick . . . bzzz, rattle, woosh. Crack [silence].

And so, the sounds of the pitching machine echoed over and over at the Harper County Bobcats batting cages. Per the coach's orders, every varsity player would take his turn at the plate with fifty swings each day after school. To pass the time, typically the guys would make a game of how many trucks they could count in the parking lot across the street. That is when their coach wasn't watching.

Occasionally the head coach would interrupt this little game with the same command. "Gentlemen, there's no value if you're just swinging a bat. Stop going through the motions. Apply some thought to what you are doing." He would follow this rebuke with three loud claps and then a large spit of sunflower seeds.

When it comes to thoughtfulness at practice, the Harper County baseball coach is not alone. Many sports coaches apply great concern toward the intentional practice of their players. But why do they have so much concern for such simple actions, like swinging a bat? For the same reason, God expressed His concern toward Judah's actions when He spoke through the Old Testament prophet in Isaiah 28:13: "And the word of the LORD will be to them precept upon precept, precept upon precept, line upon line, line upon line, here a little, there a little, that they may go, and fall backward, and be broken, and snared, and taken." That verse might come off as a bit confusing, but a little context will help.

In Isaiah 28 the Lord pronounced judgment on Judah's rebellion. He condemned Judah because His teaching had become meaningless to them. The phrases "precept upon precept, precept upon precept, line upon line, line upon line, here a little, there a little" are used by God to describe Judah as children who are repeatedly taught the same lesson but aren't learning anything. God is exposing Judah's spiritual dullness by saying they only go through the motions.

Unfortunately, this is the same trap many believers fall into today. They treat their faith much like the baseball guys treated batting practice. Bible reading, check. Prayer time, check. Verse of the Day, check. The list goes on and on as we check the boxes of our religious routine. No doubt, it's far less mentally taxing to go through the motions than actually applying effort toward spiritual disciplines, but that is not how God intends His relationship with you to work.

In the same way that God sought a genuine relationship with the children of Judah. God seeks a genuine relationship with you. That relationship is not built around mindless activities you're rushing to get done. God has provided the means to deepen your relationship with Him in prayer and Bible reading, but you must do them intentionally.

APPLICATION:

Pick a time this week to spend with God. Don't count it as your Bible study or prayer time, and don't come into the time with an agenda of how you will spend it. Simply grab your Bible, find a place that is distraction-free (leaving behind any electronic devices that could disturb you), and let God lead the time however He chooses.

TIP:

Ideally, choose a point of your day that won't require you to set a limit for how long your time with God will last.

HARD DAY AT PRACTICE

The similarities between twin brothers C. J. and Brady were uncanny. Both grew up in the same New York home, were the same size, and had the same dream: to be the world's greatest boxer. However, by the time the two reached age seventeen, differences were starting to emerge between the two high school seniors. When the twins had first started boxing, they made a family decision that training in separate gyms would be best for the both of them. As a result of this choice, every day after school C. J. would make his way to Uptown Boxing Academy while Brady trained at Parker Street Boxing Club. At first this seemed like a minor variance for the brothers. What they didn't realize was the drastic difference in coaching the two would receive.

C. J. had a coach much older than Brady's, who was always concerned about discipline. C. J. often came home after practice describing how his coach would stress staying disciplined in the ring, in training, and even at school. Brady, on the other hand, had a much looser coach. Brady's coach was more focused on the way Brady looked and felt in the ring.

Over the years this seemingly minor difference ultimately led to two completely different outcomes. C. J.'s disciplined approach allowed him to maximize his athletic potential and go on to become the first New Yorker to win a United States Boxing Championship— while Brady became rather lax about boxing and let his talent go to waste. He ended up struggling in amateur competition until deciding to hang up his gloves altogether.

Two boxers. Similar starting points. One big difference. Here's where the story ties into your faith. In the New Testament, Hebrews 12:5-6 tell us, "My son, do not regard lightly the discipline of the Lord, nor be weary when reproved by him. For the Lord disciplines the one he loves, and chastises every son whom he receives." The message from these verses is clear: God is a loving Father Who disciplines His children.

What's important to note here is that God's discipline will not always be a consequence for sin. Many Christians falsely assume that all discipline coming from God is a consequence for doing wrong, but that isn't the case. At times God will allow His children to go through hardships for the purpose of increased spiritual training. C. J.'s coach is a practical example of this. C. J. was not receiving consequences for doing wrong when his coach placed an increased emphasis on discipline; C. J. was simply being physically trained. God works in the same way, which leads us back to the beginning.

Similar to the twin brothers' decision to train in two separate gyms, you also have a decision to make. Are you willing to receive the Lord's discipline as He lovingly works to train you for greater growth of godliness, or will you disregard the Lord's discipline in favor of a looser lifestyle, more focused on how you look and feel? The decision is yours: which gym will you train in?

APPLICATION:

A significant first step toward living a disciplined life is understanding how to appropriately respond to God's discipline. Try reading the full context from the passage above, found in Hebrews 12:1–13. You may find it helpful to focus especially on verses 11–13, which provide guidance for how to respond to God's discipline.

TIP:

Although you might not be going through a hardship at the moment, keep in mind that God is still calling you to live a disciplined life through study and obedience to His Word.

PRACTICE

AFTER A MORNING PRACTICE

The next time you find yourself in a grocery store, take a stroll down the cereal aisle and see if you can find one of the most iconic breakfast cereals of all time: "Wheaties: The Breakfast of Champions."

Since the origin of Wheaties, General Mills has been a trendsetter in its rather outside-of-the-box approach to the famed breakfast cereal. Originally gaining popularity through a radio jingle, the company made a move in 1958 that would forever change the direction of the cereal when it featured Olympian Bob Richards on the front cover.[31] Since that time, athletes across America have grown up starting their day with the power-packed whole wheat flakes found inside the Wheaties box, all while dreaming of one day adorning the cover themselves.

When it comes to athletics and cereal, Wheaties tops the list. With many of the greatest athletes to ever live finding their way on the cover, Wheaties will always be "The Breakfast of Champions." Although Wheaties and the Scriptures may sound like two wildly different topics, they intersect on one significant point: they fuel champions.

Jesus picked up on this point in Matthew 4:4 when He said, "Man shall not live by bread alone, but by every word that comes from the mouth of God." In this verse Jesus drew the connection between our physical well-being and our spiritual well-being. Comparable to how our bodies need food, so do our spirits. That's why 1 Peter 2:2 says, "Like newborn infants, long for the pure spiritual milk, that by it you may grow up into salvation." Together, these verses convey the great need of every Christian for the spiritual bread and milk of the Word of God.

When it comes to spiritual food, what Wheaties is to champions the Word of God is to the Christian life. Featuring within its pages many of the most recognizable Christians to ever live, the Word of

55

God is power-packed with the same truths that these iconic Bible figures used to fuel their own Christian journey. If you're looking for fuel to help you champion your Christian life, look no further than God's Word: The Book of Champions.

APPLICATION:

Messages like this can serve as a great reminder to spend more time in God's Word. However, they can also create a burdensome feeling that guilt-trips you into reluctantly extending your Bible-reading time. Rather than trying to forcefully extend your Bible time, simply incorporate it at moments that are already available, as when you're eating snacks or meals. When sitting down to eat, use the opportunity to set aside lesser activities in favor of opening the Word of God. Can you imagine what would happen if you ate as much spiritual food as physical food?

TIP:

If you struggle with reading, try listening to an audio version of the Bible instead. You can find many free recorded versions of the Bible online or in the app store.

MID-SEASON BOREDOM

When Tim, a high school freshman, walked into the first day of strength and conditioning class, he got some strange looks. Since he was four feet ten and barely tipped the scales at ninety-five pounds, everyone assumed "Little T" was in the wrong class. At the start of the year Tim could barely bench the bar, and he certainly wasn't going to put any weight on it. But to the surprise of everyone, including the coaches, Tim didn't drop the class. He kept showing up for every workout and continued pushing himself all year.

Three years later when Tim walked into the strength and conditioning class on the first day of his senior year, he once again attracted much attention. This time it was for a different reason. Tim was the previous year's powerlifting state champion. As Tim began his usual warm-up, everyone watched as a timid and scrawny underclassman walked up to the powerlifting champion to ask him a question.

After tapping Tim on his impressively large biceps, the underclassman stammered, "Uh, Tim, does it ever get easier?"

Everyone watched silently as Tim replied. "No, but you get stronger."

Let's pause on that simple statement. What Tim said is true not only in the weight room but also of your faith. It's okay to admit that at specific points in our faith we have much the same question as the timid and scrawny underclassman: "Does this Christian thing ever get easier?" But it's in moments like that when it's critical to remember what the Scriptures have to say in response to this matter. In Philippians 2:12–13 we read, "Therefore, my beloved, as you have always obeyed, so now, not only as in my presence but much more in my absence, work out your own salvation with fear and trembling, for it is God who works in you, both to will and to work for his good pleasure."

This verse is a command with confidence. Believers are commanded to work out their faith while providing confidence that God is behind the work.

With this truth in mind, let's draw our minds back to the story of Tim. When Tim first started lifting weights, it didn't take much to challenge him physically. Yet as Tim grew stronger, he was forced to add more weight to the bar to continue improving. The same is true with your faith. When you first became a believer, it might not have taken much to challenge you spiritually. But now that you are further along in your walk with God, it's important that you continue pushing yourself for even spiritual growth. Things won't get easier, but by God's grace you will become stronger.

APPLICATION:

Use this week as an opportunity to look for ways to challenge your faith. This might mean getting more involved in a local youth group or setting your alarm ten minutes earlier for more time in God's Word. Whatever you choose, remember it's supposed to be out of your comfort zone. If the thought of it makes you feel a little uneasy, you've probably found the right thing.

TIP:

When looking for areas of your faith to grow in, consider challenging any faith-based activities that you have kept the same way for an extended period of time. For example, if your morning prayer time has been five minutes for the past three years, it's probably time to try bumping it up to ten minutes.

MAKING SACRIFICES

American distance runner Steve Prefontaine may be one of the greatest runners you've never heard of. Dying tragically in a car accident at the young age of twenty-four, Pre, as he was more commonly known, made a mark on the running community that continued well past his death.[32] Remembered by many loyal followers for his grit, determination, and work ethic, he embodied sacrifice—a word that rings back to one of Pre's most legendary quotes: "To give anything less than your best is to sacrifice the gift."[33]

Sacrifice is an act that is almost universally looked upon in a positive light. From the world of sports to the domain of faith, in the minds of many, being one who sacrifices often places you on an elevated level. But have you ever stopped to ask why sacrifice is such a good thing? For a Christian, the Bible gives the answer to that question.

Let's begin by looking at Philippians 3:8, where the apostle Paul said, "Indeed, I count everything as loss because of the surpassing worth of knowing Christ Jesus my Lord. For his sake I have suffered the loss of all things and count them as rubbish, in order that I may gain Christ." In this passage Paul was making a bold claim about sacrifice. His point was that his focus wasn't on the sacrifices he made but on Christ, Whom he was gaining. This was the same reasoning that Jesus brilliantly explained in the form of two back-to-back parables. They are found in Matthew 13:44–46: "The kingdom of heaven is like treasure hidden in a field, which a man found and covered up. Then in his joy he goes and sells all that he has and buys that field. Again, the kingdom of heaven is like a merchant in search of fine pearls, who, on finding one pearl of great value, went and sold all that he had and bought it."

Once again, these verses bring clarity to our question from the beginning. When Paul and Jesus spoke about the good of sacrifice, they weren't concentrating on the sacrifices themselves but on a reward that is far better. This brings us back to Pre's words.

When Pre powerfully proclaimed, "To give anything less than your best is to sacrifice the gift," he was onto something. Although the runner was referring to sports, at the heart of Pre's quote is a message that runs deep. To not sacrifice is to sacrifice what is best. You may have to think about that for a moment. In essence, you will always be making a sacrifice—whether that sacrifice means giving up your comforts and pleasure for what's best, or on the flip side, giving up what's best for your comforts and pleasures.

As Christians we can often focus our attention on all that we are called to give up—inappropriate jokes, foul language, reckless partying, and the like. But when those sacrifices are put up against what we have to gain, the comparison isn't even worth making. The question is: what do you want to sacrifice?

APPLICATION:

Challenge yourself to step away from one form of media for a full week. That could be a social media platform, streaming service, or other media you spend your free time on. Preferably, your chosen media should be one that you use most often. Once you've settled on a specific form, pick a more profitable activity to replace it with. This could be anything from spending time with family to going on a walk.

TIP:

On the final day of your "media fast," use your free time to review your experience. What did you like about it? What did you miss? Answering questions like these can be helpful in making changes moving forward.

FACING THE FEAR OF OTHERS

It's time to test your trivia skills. Try answering the three following true-or-false questions:

1. The world's largest jumbotron is found in the AT&T Stadium, home of the Dallas Cowboys.
   a. True
   b. False

2. Powering a World Cup soccer match can take up to 25,000 kWh of energy. (Hint, a regular household lamp requires 0.06 kWh.[34])
   a. True
   b. False

3. In a standard gymnasium, the brightest light is typically the scoreboard possession indicator, estimated at 1,700 lumens.
   a. True
   b. False

(Before you continue, check your responses with the answer key at the end of this devotion.)

Now that you've learned the answers to our trivia questions, we can focus our attention on how the Scriptures relate to the third question. We'll start by looking at a rather popular passage of Scripture found in Matthew 5:14–16, in which Jesus said, "You are the light of the world. A city set on a hill cannot be hidden. Nor do people light a lamp and put it under a basket, but on a stand, and it gives light to all in the house. In the same way, let your light shine before others, so that they may see your good works and give glory to your Father who is in heaven."

Jesus's words in this passage bring to light an incredible truth. As a Christian, you should be the brightest light in the stadium, on the court, or wherever you practice and play your sport. Nothing should outshine you. Unfortunately, this can sometimes prove to be quite a challenge.

Often the dark influence of the environments we find ourselves in can be very difficult to conquer. Thankfully, you need only to consider where your source of power comes from to overcome this darkness. Christ! The power you need to shine your light isn't something you have to provide yourself; the source—Jesus—is already in you. It's not your job to create the light; it's simply your job to shine.

APPLICATION:

The thought of shining your light for Christ may still seem intimidating, but taking a first step can be rather simple. Begin every practice by asking God to open your eyes to the opportunities for sharing your faith that surround you. When those opportunities provide themselves, rest in the understanding that the power to shine is already inside you.

TIP:

You're not alone when it comes to battling the fear of others. Even the apostle Paul asked others to pray for his boldness in Ephesians 6:18–20.

---

1. *True:* AT&T Stadium boasts the world's largest jumbotron, containing over thirty million LEDs and 25,000 square feet of video displays.[35]

2. *True:* A 90-minute World Cup soccer match can consume up to 25,000 kWh of energy; that's enough wattage to power over a dozen houses for an entire year.[36]

3. *False:* The brightest light in any sports setting should be a Christian. (Continue with the rest of the devotion.)

FEELING DISCOURAGED

Dick Hoyt and Rick Hoyt were a rather inspirational sight to see as they lined up on the starting line of the 2014 Boston Marathon. Having already completed the race thirty-one times,[37] it wasn't simply the father and son's presence that made the duo inspiring, but the story of how they got there.

Shortly after his birth, the son, Rick Hoyt, was diagnosed with a severe form of cerebral palsy. Suffering significant physical and mental disabilities due to his condition, Rick was left wheelchair-bound for his entire life. Unable to walk or run, road races appeared as an impossibility for Rick until his nineteenth birthday, when he had an idea. Motivated by a benefit run, Rick asked his father, Dick, to cover the five-mile distance pushing him in his wheelchair.

With Dick having agreed to the request, the unlikely pair showed up on race day and together made their way through the file-mile course, not knowing that race would only be the beginning of their career. Competing in more than 1,000 races over the course of a thirty-year span, the father-son team could be found at countless races, competing side-by-side from start to finish.[38] Their final major race was completed by crossing the 2014 Boston Marathon finish line in 7:37:33 for the thirty-second time.[39]

The story of Dick and Rick paints a heart-warming picture of fatherly affection and loyal love—two qualities that find their greatest expressions in God's relationship with His children. We see this wonderfully demonstrated in Joshua 1:9: "Have I not commanded you? Be strong and courageous. Do not be frightened, and do not be dismayed, for the LORD your God is with you wherever you go." Those words are as true today as they were in Joshua's day, and they hold the same comforting thought that is echoed in Hebrews 13:5–6, when God said, "'I will never leave you nor forsake you.' So we can confidently say, 'The Lord is my helper; I will not fear; what can man do to me?'" What these verses draw to mind is a picture of God's extraordinary relationship with you.

Closely resembling the unbroken bond between Dick and Rick as they raced side by side every step of the Boston Marathon is God's bond with you. Your relationship as a child of God will continue unbroken as He remains by your side, every step of your race of faith. Although your feelings can sometimes betray you, that does not mean God has abandoned you. You can be confident that your heavenly Father will "never leave you nor forsake you."

APPLICATION:

During times of discouragement, sitting alone in silence can sound less than appealing, but it is often a helpful practice. Find a quiet spot to take some time and meditate on God's Word. Pick a verse, ideally one from above, and think through each word deeply and carefully. As you meditate on the words, try answering these questions:

- What is being said in the passage?
- What does it mean?
- What does this passage teach me about God?
- What effect should this have on my life?

TIP:

Christian meditation is vastly different than eastern meditation. Christian mediation is focused on filling your mind, while eastern mediation is focused on emptying your mind.

GOING THROUGH A TRIAL

On March 30, 1986, under the shining lights of Rupp Arena in Lexington, Kentucky, the Texas Longhorns women's basketball team capped off a historic 34–0 season with their national championship win against the USC Trojans.[40] In this victory the Longhorns succeeded in a feat previously unheard of in women's college basketball: having an undefeated season—an accomplishment that has forever marked the program as being the first women's college basketball team to do so.[41]

Undefeated. Even the word has a special ring to it. There's an attractive charm to the idea of having a perfect record—one that inspires countless athletes to pursue the accomplishment every year. Nevertheless, it's rare for an athlete to ever get a taste of what perfection feels like, as the large majority of competitors will face the dread of defeat at least at one point throughout their season.

The theme of remaining undefeated and the disappointment that comes with defeat are not exclusive to the world of sports. As Christians, we often consider many of the everyday trials we face as interruptions to our desire for a victorious life of faith . . . but we don't have to.

In the Scriptures a promise is given to God's children guaranteeing an undefeated status. The promise is found in Romans 8:35–37: "Who shall separate us from the love of Christ? Shall tribulation, or distress, or persecution, or famine, or nakedness, or danger, or sword? As it is written, 'For your sake we are being killed all the day long; we are regarded as sheep to be slaughtered.' No, in all these things we are more than conquerors through him who loved us." There's a powerful lesson behind the words "more than conquerors" that we don't want to miss. Let's consider what that phrase means.

In this verse the word *conquer* means to "come off victorious."[42] Yet notice that the verse doesn't simply describe you as a conqueror but rather a "more than" conqueror. In other words, it's promising to make you "more than" victorious. How is that possible? The answer is tremendously inspiring. To be more than victorious means you don't just beat your opponent but that your opponent becomes the very thing that benefits you. In other words, these verses are promising that Christ gives you the ability to not only defeat the difficulties that you're facing but also to use those difficulties for your own eternal good.

As a Christian, whether you are facing a trial or a setback, a failure or a defeat, whatever may be trying to drag your faith down can actually work to push your faith to greater heights. It might be hard to see now, but in whatever circumstances you find yourself and however difficult it may be, remember who Christ has made you to be—more than a conqueror! Through Christ you are undefeated.

APPLICATION:

Keeping a daily journal is an excellent tool for seeing God's faithfulness throughout your life. Over the next month, try logging a personal journal each day. This entry could be as short or as long as you like and can be written in any format that you prefer (such as, paper or digital). At the start of the following month, reread each journal entry on the day it falls. (For example, January 1 would be read on February 1, and so on.) As you look back, you will likely see many of the ways God was working in the past that you couldn't see at that moment.

TIP:

If you're a guy, you might raise a few objections over the idea of journaling. Setting aside those hesitations will be well worth seeing God's faithfulness more clearly in your life.

CONVICTED OVER SIN

A large crowd of bewildered fans funneled through the gymnasium exits, stunned by what had happened. With twenty-five seconds to go, the Hooverville High girls varsity basketball team was ahead by three, with Brooklyn, the starting point guard, eyeing her competitor in a low defensive position. What started as aggressive defense ended with a reach-in foul that Brooklyn clearly disagreed with. Enraged by the official's whistle, Brooklyn burst into an angry rant, giving full vent to her emotions until a technical foul was stacked onto her penalty. Being pulled from the game and seated on the bench, Brooklyn watched as the opposing team was granted two free throws and possession of the ball, an opportunity they capitalized on. After sinking both free throws, the opposing offense carefully executed a pick-and-roll play to score an open layup and deal the Hooverville girls a bitter defeat.

Moments after the shocking conclusion, Brooklyn slowly made her way over to her coach. Gazing at his feet and with tears streaming down her bright red cheeks, Brooklyn choked out the words, "I'm sorry." Time seemed to stop as Brooklyn lifted her head, expecting a sympathetic response. Instead, she saw a stern, irritated stare and two firmly crossed arms.

At this point, this situation might appear as if a heartless coach was making a traumatic experience even more tragic. However, a little background on the situation can change that perspective. This was not the first time Brooklyn had led her team to defeat because of an outrage. If truth be told, it was the third game that year Brooklyn allowed her emotions to get the best of her, leading to a loss. Brooklyn's coach wasn't heartless; he simply didn't believe the words coming out of her mouth.

As we consider this situation, let's look at 2 Corinthians 7:10–11, which says, "For godly grief produces a repentance that leads to salvation without regret, whereas worldly grief produces death. For see what earnestness this godly grief has produced in you, but also what eagerness to clear yourselves, what indignation, what fear, what longing, what zeal, what punishment! At every point you have proved yourselves innocent in the matter." These verses explain that feeling bad about something and truly repenting are two completely different things. Our story about Brooklyn provides an excellent example of this.

When Brooklyn apologized to her coach, her words lacked all meaning because she had chosen to make the same mistake over and over again. Similarly, as a Christian, it can often be easy to fall into the trap of offering God a quick and meaningless "Please forgive me" prayer after you sin. Although you might feel bad because you've sinned, it doesn't become true repentance until you change.

APPLICATION:

If you have sinned, confessing your wrong to God is a significant first step. But it shouldn't stop there. Second Corinthians 7:10–11 offers a list of key markers that demonstrate true repentance. Consider if you see these qualities in your own life:

- Earnestness/eagerness: a diligence to prove that you've changed and to remain that way
- Indignation/fear: a feeling of anger toward the sin you have committed and a fear of repeating it
- Longing/zeal/punishment: an aching pursuit for the sin to be resolved, whatever the consequences

TIP:

If you have truly repented, the next step is to truly rejoice! (See Psalm 103:8–14).

STANDING UP AGAINST BULLYING

Aloud noise signaled the end of the school day. Lamar quickly grabbed his book bag and made his way down the hall into the locker room to get changed for practice. As he opened his locker and began to take out his gear, Lamar overheard some senior football players jeering back and forth with nasty comments directed at a freshman. Before long things started to get out of hand, and one of the senior players took the lead in a full-blown verbal assault.

"Ha, I wouldn't get playing time either if my grandma could beat me in an arm-wrestling match."

"I bet he still wears tighty whities," another added.

As Lamar glanced over at the scene, it became apparent that tears were welling up in the scrawny freshman's eyes, who was now trembling in a corner.

"Well, let's just find out," announced the bully as he rushed to pull down the freshman's athletic shorts.

Before he could get a firm-enough grip to expose the helpless freshmen, the noise of a toilet flushing and a stall door opening interrupted the commotion. Silence struck the locker room full of high schoolers as the head football coach walked out from behind the stall door. Stunned, everyone froze as they anticipated what would happen next.

As awful as this locker room situation is, it's not uncommon for episodes like this to occur regularly. Unfortunately, the locker room has often become a place where sin runs unchecked in the hearts of many. For a Christian, this must not be the case.

In the Old Testament book of Proverbs, a book devoted to teaching wisdom, we find this warning in Proverbs 15:3: "The eyes of the LORD are in every place, keeping watch on the evil and the good." Those words may place the fear of God in your heart, and they're meant to. However, as powerful as those words are, the book of Matthew takes this matter a step further. In Matthew 28:20 Jesus declares to His followers: "And behold, I am with you always, to the end of the age." Here's the sobering reality. As a Christian, when you walk into the locker room, Jesus walks in with you.

If the presence of a coach can change how bullies act, how much more should the Lord's presence change how you act? You might not be able to control the circumstances of the locker room, but those circumstances don't need to control you. God is watching. Jesus is with you. Never forget that.

APPLICATION:

Think of a teammate who would be willing to stand with you against sin in the locker room. The next time you see this teammate, ask if he or she would commit to backing you up in the locker room when difficult situations present themselves (such as, defending the helpless, refusing to join in on bullying, and so on). This commitment should go two ways, both when you need to be bold against wrongdoing and when they do.

TIP:

Ideally your chosen teammate will be a fellow Christian.

FRUSTRATED WITH A TEAMMATE

It was Sunday evening and Cameron was in the zone, diligently working on his homework until a yell from the other room startled him. Curious about the uproar, Cameron wandered through the hallway into the TV room and found a familiar scene unfolding. Seated on the edge of the couch with his elbows on his knees was Cameron's older brother, Zeke, who was staring intently at the television. Zeke's favorite NBA team had started playing, and Cameron knew what that meant. Zeke would take it upon himself to coach the team from their family couch the entire game. Cameron returned to his room as more cries erupted.

"C'mon—that was an absolute freebee he missed!"

"Would you just run the play and stop trying to show off!"

"Who even is number 13? Sit him on the bench!"

In most sporting environments the situation described is not out of the ordinary. It's a common practice for many devoted fans to take on the role of couch coach as they loudly express their opinions about the performance of their favorite players. The attitude behind this critiquing fits well alongside one of Jesus's more popular teachings from Matthew 7:1–5.

> *Judge not, that you be not judged. For with the judgment you pronounce, you will be judged, and with the measure you use it will be measured to you. Why do you see the speck that is in your brother's eye, but do not notice the log that is in your own eye? Or how can you say to your brother, "Let me take the speck out of your eye," when there is the log in your own eye? You hypocrite, first take the log out of your own eye, and then you will see clearly to take the speck out of your brother's eye.*

A lot could be said about these few verses, but we will focus our attention on one central point: spiritual criticism. Comparable to a devoted fan who sits back and nitpicks the performance of his favorite players, it can be far too easy to take this same approach when it comes to your faith. As Christians, our lives should not be spent constantly analyzing the spiritual performance of others. Instead, our focus is much better directed toward Christ, specifically loving and serving Him.

Although every single person will be judged one day, all will be judged by God and His standards, not by you and your own personal preferences. When you're more concerned about the actions of the next person than you are your own, you're playing the role of God.

APPLICATION:

Make a habit of complimenting one teammate before every practice. As you form this routine, do your best to give genuine, meaningful compliments rather than artificial, petty ones. For example, a compliment such as "I admire the hustle you give out on the court" can go a lot further than simply saying, "You're doing good."

TIP:

Actively look for admirable qualities in your teammates that you can compliment them on.

BURDENED BEYOND BEARING

It's called the "Atlas Stones." Renowned in the World's Strongest Man competition as a marquee event,[43] competitors are challenged with a daunting task. Lift five stones from the ground, hoist each onto a platform, and do it as quickly as possible. The catch: the stones range in weight from 310 to 440 pounds.[44] Having gained notoriety for its impressive feat of strength, the Atlas Stones portray a vivid image of how you may feel when experiencing the burdens of life. It's as though you've come upon boulders much too heavy to lift and need the world's strongest man to move them. In instances like this, the Scriptures give believers the direction they need.

Found within the thirty-seventh Psalm are the words of David, a man who was familiar with the extremes of existence. From running for his life to reigning as king, David was a man who knew the weight of life's burdens, and in Psalm 37:5 he offered a simple but profound solution: "Commit your way to the LORD; trust in him, and he will act." Expressed in this verse are three powerful statements, the first of which can have even greater weightiness if we examine it a little more closely.

In the ancient Hebrew the word for *commit* was literally *roll*.[45] Drawing from this concept, the verse carries the idea of rolling onto the Lord the burden of your life circumstances, trusting Him and then watching God do what you can't. David was making the point that you can avoid a lot of unnecessary suffering when you roll the burdens of your life to God rather than trying to lift them yourself. Which brings the Atlas Stones back to mind.

Today you may find yourself in a situation that seems as if you've been entered into the Atlas Stones competition. You feel as if you are standing in front of giant stones with no way of moving them. Don't lose heart—there is One Who can. The God of all strength is ready to bear your burdens if you will roll them to Him and trust Him to act.

APPLICATION:

Sometimes, prayer can be hard. You don't know what to say or how to say it. That's why writing out your prayers can be a helpful way to thoughtfully express your heart to God. Take a moment to sit down and write out a heartfelt prayer. As you do, you may find it useful to think through the following questions:

1. What burdens am I currently facing?

2. How do I feel about these burdens? Why do I feel this way?

3. What do I know to be true about God? How should that impact my response to these burdens?

Keep in mind that many Psalms are simply prayers recorded in the Scriptures.

TIP:

If writing out your prayers is a habit you want to form, consider buying a journal to keep all your written prayers in one place.

MISSED A PRACTICE

At some point in your athletic career, it's likely that you have, or will, come across the popular slogan EAT. TRAIN. SLEEP. REPEAT. It's the mentality of a champion, right? Maybe in the world's eyes, but the slogan is far from the truth in God's kingdom. In fact, it serves as a great starting point for an incredibly important topic that any Christian athlete must consider. That's the topic of idolatry.

The Bible has much to say about idolatry as it relates to all areas of life, including sports. One of the many warnings about the danger of idolatry is found in 1 Corinthians 6:12: "'All things are lawful for me,' but not all things are helpful. 'All things are lawful for me,' but I will not be dominated by anything." Notice this verse is not saying God is the only good thing. It's pointing out the reality that good things become bad things when they take the place of God in your life. Simply put, an idol is anything that steals your heart from God.

This message is not new to God's people. Way back in the Old Testament book of Exodus, God provided the Ten Commandments for His chosen people to follow. Do you know what topped the list? It's found in Exodus 20:3: "You shall have no other gods before me." Once again, it's a warning against the danger of idolatry.

Sadly, we live in a world that has elevated sports to the level of a god. The good news is that sports don't have to operate this way. The bad news is that you live in a culture that pressures you to let them. Phrases like EAT. TRAIN. SLEEP. REPEAT. may initially appear innocent, but they hide a deadly mentality for any Christian to accept.

If your sport has become an idol, it will be necessary for you to humbly readjust your heart to keep God first. In doing this, you can be confident that you will enjoy your sport much more when you're not looking for it to fulfill the role of God in your life.

APPLICATION:

Take a moment to answer the following questions:

- Would you consider your entire day a waste if you didn't have practice or a game?
- Do you have to play your sport to be in a good mood?
- Does your sport get in the way of obeying God?

If you answered yes to any of these questions, it might be time to reconsider the place your sport has taken in your heart.

TIP:

Instead of being frustrated when you miss a practice or competition, look for ways you can spend the extra time growing in your relationship with Christ.

FEELING STUCK IN YOUR ROUTINE

When the original hit action drama *The Karate Kid* swept across theaters in 1984, countless hearts were moved by the inspirational story. Set in sunny Los Angeles, California, the storyline follows Daniel LaRusso as he makes his rise from being the easy target for school bullies to the Under 18 All-Valley Karate Champion.[46] Central to the film's plot is a key scene when Daniel loses patience with his teacher, Mr. Miyagi. Having come to Mr. Miyagi to learn karate, Daniel complained that all Mr. Miyagi had done was use his pupil to sand his decks, wax his car, and paint his house.

Unmoved by the teenager's irritations, Mr. Miyagi calmly turned to his student and demanded that he replicate the movements he was so familiar with. "Show me sand the floor," Mr. Miyagi ordered.

Much to Daniel's startlement, each of the activities Mr. Miyagi had his pupil repeating were actually karate moves. When Mr. Miyagi finally began throwing punches and kicks at Daniel near the end of the scene, Daniel's reflexes were so agile that he could hardly believe it himself.[47]

Karate Kid. Mr. Miyagi. Faith. These three things tie together exceptionally well when it comes to the topic of God's faithfulness. Here's how: In the Scriptures we find many examples of God's faithfulness. From the promises to Abraham to the birth of the Messiah, God has always shown Himself to be faithful—a quality that 1 Corinthians 1:9 makes plain and clear: "God is faithful, by whom you were called into the fellowship of his Son, Jesus Christ our Lord." The first phrase of that verse is simple enough. Yet 2 Timothy 2:13 takes things a step further: "If we are faithless, [God] remains faithful—for he cannot deny himself." Together, these two verses remind us that God will not change from being Who He is: faithful.

Sometimes in our Christian lives it can feel as if we're LaRusso, stuck in the same old boring routine and getting tired of it. If we're being honest, it can be easy to believe the lie that God has you in a pointless situation doing things that have no value. Thankfully, that will never be the case. God is similar to Mr. Miyagi in that He always has a reason for where He has you and what He has you doing. Like LaRusso, you might not always see those reasons, but have no doubt—you can always trust God's faithfulness. The entire Bible is evidence of God's faithfulness that climaxes with the cross of Christ.

If God was faithful to send His Son to die on the cross, do you think He would be unfaithful in any other way? When frustrations and boredom come knocking at your door, the answer is to look to the cross and ask yourself, "Is God not faithful?" Keep the phrase "Look to the cross" in your back pocket for situations that require your trust in God.

APPLICATION:

The idea of "looking to the cross" is symbolic, but it can have a physical component if you would like. Look around your house and see if you can find an unused cross you can place somewhere you will see it regularly. If you don't have one, you can try looking online for one to purchase. Use it as a physical reminder that God is faithful and can be trusted wherever He has you.

TIP:

If you don't have a cross, countless other cross-based items can be equally effective in serving as a reminder (such as a, necklace, phone wallpaper, and so on).

GETTING HOME FROM PRACTICE

Imagine that it's a regular weekday, and you're finally making it home after a long day at school. As you walk in the door, you're surprised to be greeted by a thick letter lying on the kitchen table with your name on it. When you open the card, a sparkling VIP pass falls out. After reading the card, you learn that one of your family members decided to buy you a ticket to attend an upcoming event where your favorite athlete is scheduled to speak. *No way!* you think. *This will be great!*

A few weeks pass, and the big night arrives. You make the trip to the enormous stadium full of attendees. This will be a night to remember. Once you find your seat, the speaker comes out on stage and the lights dim. You can hardly believe your eyes. *It's them.*

Before you know it, the speech is over, and you are being led with a group of other VIPs to the backstage area for an opportunity to talk with the speaker. As you stand in line you begin to sweat. Your hands are getting cold, and your stomach starts to flutter. You didn't expect to get this nervous, so you try to calm yourself with deep, slow breaths. When the large straight-faced bodyguard calls your name, you take a step forward into the presence of your hero and stand awe-struck. *I can't believe this is really happening.*

Let's stop there. You're probably getting the idea. Although the thought of something like this ever happening might sound completely impractical, the idea behind it relates to both you and the Scriptures. In Isaiah 6:1–5 we encounter a vision that the Old Testament prophet Isaiah had of God's throne room. Isaiah recounts his vision in this way:

> *In the year that King Uzziah died I saw the Lord*
> *sitting upon a throne, high and lifted up; and the*
> *train of his robe filled the temple. Above him stood*

*the seraphim. Each had six wings: with two he cov-
ered his face, and with two he covered his feet, and
with two he flew. And one called to another and
said: "Holy, holy, holy is the L*ORD* of hosts; the whole
earth is full of his glory!" And the foundations of the
thresholds shook at the voice of him who called, and
the house was filled with smoke. And I said: "Woe
is me! For I am lost; for I am a man of unclean lips,
and I dwell in the midst of a people of unclean lips;
for my eyes have seen the King, the L*ORD* of hosts!"*

Isaiah was taken aback by the magnificence of the throne room
of God, and his experience has implications for your own life. These
verses give believers a glimpse of what it would be like to be in the
throne room of God—a place you enter every time you pray.

Although meeting your sports hero in the way suggested at the
beginning may be unreasonable, meeting with the God of the universe is not. When you pray you enter the throne room of God. You
may not see what Isaiah did, but the reality is still the same.

APPLICATION:

Next time you're getting ready to pray, take a moment to pause
and think about Who you will be approaching. Use this time to
set your mind in the right place before speaking with God. Although the idea of pre-prayer preparation may be unfamiliar
to you, begin to work at making a regular practice of properly
aligning your thoughts before prayer.

TIP:

As alarming as Isaiah's vision is, you don't have to approach
God's throne room in fear. Check out Hebrews 4:14–16 to
learn why.

SERVING YOUR TEAMMATES

You are about to enter the mind of ninth-grader Jasmine Heart. She is a five-feet-six-inch, blonde-haired, brown-eyed freshman at Valley Center High in Cleveland, Ohio. She enjoys creative activities like art and music, and her favorite class is science. Jasmine is known by her friends for her Christian beliefs and often attends activities at her local church. Going into her first year of high school, Jasmine decided to try out for tennis. This decision presented her with a brand-new set of challenges she hadn't faced in middle school.

One day early in the season, Jasmine walked into the locker room after practice to find an absolute mess. She had stayed late to practice her serve technique with the coach and was the last girl left at school. Standing at the door, Jasmine scanned the chaos and began to think, *I should pick up the locker room for the girls tonight!* Jasmine stood shining with a bright, white smile, preparing to act until more thoughts flooded her mind. *Well, maybe that's a good idea, but that would reinforce a bad habit in others.* She paused. *Plus, that's what they pay the janitor for anyway.* Jasmine's smile began to droop. *And now that I think about it, I don't even know where to put everything.* Now glaring at the mess with a blank, uninterested stare, Jasmine walked to her locker, got her bag, and left.

Jasmine's story conveys the tragic fate of many good intentions. What may initially seem like a good idea can often be drowned in a flood of excuses before it sees the light of day. Undoubtedly, this is often because it can be much easier to come up with reasons for not serving others than reasons for serving. But not so fast. The Scriptures clearly provide the answer to these excuses with a simple reason to act. That reason is found in 2 Corinthians 9:8: "And God is able to make all grace abound to you, so that having all sufficiency in all things at all times, you may abound in every good work." Paul's encouragement in this verse for doing good works is clear: God can provide all you need for every good work.

Like our story with Jasmine, excuses tend to outweigh intentions when it comes to acts of service. This is unfortunate because the best intentions that don't happen will never beat the smallest acts of service that do. When you have a good intention, act on it. The reason is simple too: God promises to provide everything you need, at all times, for every good work.

APPLICATION:

Quickly brainstorm one specific way to serve a teammate tomorrow. This could be anything from writing him or her an encouraging note to bringing that person a sports drink before practice. Once you've settled on your act of service, determine that no excuses will keep you from fulfilling your chosen act when the time comes tomorrow.

TIP:

Don't overthink the concept of service. Be willing to act upon good intentions as they come to you throughout the day.

WATCHING YOUR WORDS

When Thomas tried out for the swim team his junior year, the swimmers knew they were in for it. Known around the school for his loose lips, Thomas had been kicked off the school basketball team his freshman year and wrestling team his sophomore year due to his foul language. Heading into the first day of practice, most of the swimmers expected that Thomas would be coming more to talk than to swim.

Their expectations were proven correct when thirty minutes into the first practice, Thomas was found bullying a first-year student about how scrawny he looked. It was no sooner than the coach had stopped the act of bullying that Thomas was on a starting block, challenging a senior to a race, boasting, "This is my first day, and I bet I could beat you with my hands tied behind my back."

For the swimmers it served as an irritating disruption to the practice. Thomas, on the other hand, appeared to be entirely in his element until midway through practice, when the coach asked him to turn in his uniform the following morning.

As pathetic as this story may sound, the heartbreaking truth is that there are many people like Thomas in the world. For that reason, Thomas is a fitting subject as we enter a sobering discussion about words.

Before you begin, it's crucial that you turn your thoughts away from anyone you might consider to be a "Thomas" and instead, focus on yourself. Jesus's words in Matthew 12:36–37 have a powerful message that will be much more useful when you relate them to your life. In this passage Jesus says, "I tell you, on the day of judgment people will give account for every careless word they speak, for by your words you will be justified, and by your words you will be condemned." Jesus's message is clear. You will have to answer for every careless word you say throughout your life. Every single one.

Although Thomas is an extreme example of careless speech, he exemplifies how we can often throw words around as though they mean nothing. This a problem of serious concern, considering that one day you will be judged for those words. Although this teaching might already be hard to swallow, it's important to recognize that your judgment will not be limited to curse words. It includes words that are simply "careless"—things like inappropriate jokes or discouraging comments.

The purpose of Jesus's instruction in this passage is not to be a killjoy. Jesus Himself, who never said one "careless word," was full of joy. In John 15:11 Jesus even went as far as to say, "These things I have spoken to you, that my joy may be in you, and that your joy may be full." Jesus's warning about the coming judgment of your words isn't intended to snuff out all your fun. (If you can't have fun without saying careless things, then that's an issue in and of itself.) Rather, Jesus's teaching has your best interests at heart, which includes your eternal future.

APPLICATION:

If you haven't been careful with what you've said recently or simply recognize that you need to pay more attention to what comes out of your mouth, it would be well worth your time to look up (and pray) the prayer in Psalm 19:14 and Psalm 141:3. These verses provide an excellent starting place for being careful with what you say.

TIP:

Pick one of the two verses mentioned above to write on a piece of paper ten times. As you do, carefully consider each of the words. Performing this activity will help commit your chosen verse to heart.

SHARING THE GOSPEL

It's believed to be the largest parade for a sporting event in history. Under the November sun in downtown Chicago, an estimated crowd of five million gathered to celebrate the 2016 World Series victory of the Chicago Cubs. The title ended a 108-year drought, during which the franchise looked as though it might never win another championship. When they did, the celebration proved to be worth the wait. With countless fans lining the streets, the World Series team made its way through the red-and-blue masses, sharing the joy of triumph as the champs.[48]

When a sports team wins a championship, it's memorable. When a professional franchise wins a championship for the first time in 108 years, it's monumental. But when Christ wins eternal victory for all who call on His name, it's world-changing. In 2 Corinthians 2:14–16 Paul declares, "But thanks be to God, who in Christ always leads us in triumphal procession, and through us spreads the fragrance of the knowledge of him everywhere. For we are the aroma of Christ to God among those who are being saved and among those who are perishing, to one a fragrance from death to death, to the other a fragrance from life to life."

The idea Paul is drawing from in this passage is one of an ancient Roman triumph, something his original readers would have been well acquainted with. In Roman culture, when a general was successful in conquest, he would return to Rome in a glorious fashion. Parading through the streets, the general and his army would spread the good news of victory to the citizens lining his way to the capital.[49]

Paul's connection between a Roman spectacle of this type and the spread of the gospel is clear. Christ's victory has welcomed us into His parade of conquest, inspiring us to spread the news of His triumph and encouraging us to call others to join in. This is, after all, what Jesus said in Mark 16:15: "Go into all the world and proclaim the gospel to the whole creation."

Comparable to the historic parade of the Cubs in 2016 is the heavenly parade of Christians awaiting the return of Christ. As a Christian, you've already been included in the celebration. With your salvation won on the cross, you now get the pleasure of sharing with Christ the joy of triumph and spreading the good news of victory.

APPLICATION:

When was the last time you shared the gospel with someone? If you have to think hard to remember, the answer is probably— too long ago. Prayerfully consider which of your teammates, classmates, or friends needs to hear the good news of Christ's victory. Ask the Lord to provide an opportunity to speak with this person about the gospel. If you feel uncomfortable sharing the gospel, you can use a helpful tool called the Romans Road. It consists of seven verses found in the book of Romans that when put together encompass the entire gospel. They are Romans 3:10, 3:23, 6:23, 5:8, 10:9–10, and 10:13.

TIP:

As you share the gospel, keep in mind that the power to save someone does not depend on your saying all the right words but on God's powerful working. (See Romans 1:16.)

NEEDING INSPIRATION

On the foggy morning of October 12, 2019, in Vienna, Austria, the stage was set for history to be made. With years of training in the books and countless hours spent preparing even the most minute details, marathoner Eliud Kipchoge stood waiting at the starting line of his biggest challenge yet.

Having already marked himself as the greatest marathon runner of all time with multiple gold medals and a world record performance, Kipchoge had accepted a new challenge in his career: to become the first person to run a marathon in under two hours—a milestone that had long been considered unbreakable and would require a pace slightly faster than 4:35 per mile for the entire 26.2 miles. With 120,000 people lining the streets and a broadcast reaching an estimated 500 million homes across the globe, the world watched as Kipchoge ran what would go down as the fastest marathon of all time. Crossing the finish line at 1:59:40.2, Eliud did what many had considered impossible.[50]

Following the race, Eliud gave one reporter insight into how he was able to push through the most difficult moments. "You need the heart to run,"[51] he said—revealing a powerful truth that finds its greatest significance when applied to your relationship with Christ.

Spread throughout the Bible are countless verses conveying the necessity of having a heart for Christ. Yet there may be few better than Acts 20:24: "But I do not account my life of any value nor as precious to myself, if only I may finish my course and the ministry that I received from the Lord Jesus, to testify to the gospel of the grace of God." In this verse Paul reveals his greatest motivation in life: his heart for Christ.

Your motivation as a Christian will inevitably come and go, but that's where having a heart for Christ comes into play. What you want at your very core is how you will choose to live. When Kipchoge was running his record-breaking marathon, he doubtlessly encountered significant fatigue. It was at those moments that he had a decision to make. Would he give up or keep going? His decision to press on returns to his earlier comment of having the heart to run. As a follower of Christ, the importance of having a heart for Christ cannot be understated. Motivation may get you started on the right path, but a heart for Christ will help keep you on it.

APPLICATION:

The key to building a heart for Christ is having a deepening appreciation for His life and death. Go back and reread the complete account of Jesus's death in Matthew 26:47–27:61. As you do, read it from the perspective of the Savior, going through everything He did for the sake of others. Keep in mind that Jesus didn't have to die on the cross; every single lash of the whip, every single second on the cross was an active choice of self-sacrifice.

TIP:

If you've already read the crucifixion account before, you may be tempted to rush through the story. Do your best to slow down and consider what it would be like to be present at the scene.

RESISTING TEMPTATION

The tragic story of Charles Brown has been forever etched into the minds of students at Lincoln High in Tallahassee, Florida. Going into his junior year, Brown had become one of the top ten quarterback recruits in the entire nation. Having received offers from the likes of Florida, Clemson, and Alabama, Brown entered his junior year with high expectations, and he did not disappoint.

He led the Lincoln Trojans to qualify for the FHSAA State Championship game with a number-one seed and multiple record-setting performances. Heading into state, things were looking bright, but everything changed the morning of the championship game. Early in the morning, news broke that Brown had been arrested the night before for possession of drugs. The number-one-ranked team in Florida had lost their star, and their star had lost his career. As the story developed in the ensuing months, it became clear that Brown's problem did not start the night before the championship.

During his court appearance, the judge questioned Brown about his drug use history. This is the transcript of his tear-filled response: "Your honor, my past with drugs began my freshman year when I was challenged by a senior on my team to smoke. I knew this decision would hurt my mom, but I desperately wanted the respect of my teammates. Thinking that smoking just once wouldn't matter much, I gave in. That day, your honor, began what has been a three-year addiction to various drugs." [Per federal law, Brown was sentenced to one year in prison.]

Although this story makes a powerful case for why a person should not do drugs, it serves as an even greater warning than this. Drugs may be addictive, but sin is even more so. And in the same way there's no "just once" with drugs, there's no such thing as one-time sins.

We see this clearly from the words of Solomon, the wisest man to ever live, when he wrote in Proverbs 6:10–11, "A little sleep, a little slumber, a little folding of the hands to rest, and poverty will come upon you like a robber, and want like an armed man." Yes, Solomon was specifically referring to laziness in these verses, but behind this warning was an equally important message: Little sins add up. Little sins lead to more sins.

The phrase "just once" can often be used when you want to justify an action or quiet your conscience, but this is a dangerous mindset to have. The lesson Brown teaches is very real. Sinning is like a drug; once you start, you want more. Even though the effects might seem minimal at first, you can be certain that they will end up changing your life. Resist the urge. Don't sin.

APPLICATION:

You're probably aware that resisting temptation is a battle all believers face. What you may not know is that sin has a progression. James 1:13–15 says, "Let no one say when he is tempted, 'I am being tempted by God,' for God cannot be tempted with evil, and he himself tempts no one. But each person is tempted when he is lured and enticed by his own desire. Then desire when it has conceived gives birth to sin, and sin when it is fully grown brings forth death." To paraphrase James, sin starts in your mind, moves to your actions, and then leaves its devastating consequences. Next time you find yourself tempted with a sinful thought, stop before it grows to be something more.

TIP:

Resisting temptation is much like giving in to temptation; it often becomes easier the more you do it.

FOLLOWING A FILM SESSION

As the Graber High girls' basketball team walked out of the computer lab following their Saturday morning film session, it was clear who had played well the night before and who hadn't. The first to exit were two starters, Sierra, the team's point guard, and Lilly, the post. Walking side by side, these bright-eyed girls excitedly chatted about their afternoon plans. Following them was Carrie, the starting shooting guard. Although she wasn't as peppy as the first two, Carrie casually walked out of the room staring at her phone screen. Finally, with the rest of the team having had time to file out, the final two starters, Breana and Monica, slowly wandered through the door. With their shoulders slumped forward and eyes down, the two girls displayed somber faces with red, puffy bags underneath their eyes.

When it comes to the film room, this story epitomizes the vast array of experiences an athlete can face. Depending on how you play, watching game film can either excite you to get back to your sport or persuade you to hide from your team. Although there are no Bible verses saying that when you make it to heaven you will review life film with God, a few passages do suggest something similar. One is found in 1 Corinthians 3:11–15:

> *For no one can lay a foundation other than that which is laid, which is Jesus Christ. Now if anyone builds on the foundation with gold, silver, precious stones, wood, hay, straw—each one's work will become manifest, for the Day will disclose it, because it will be revealed by fire, and the fire will test what sort of work each one has done. If the work that anyone has built on the foundation survives, he will receive a reward. If anyone's work is burned up, he will suffer loss, though he himself will be saved, but only as through fire.*

In these few verses Paul relayed a sobering message to the Corinthian church: one day they would be judged—and if you're a Christian, that means you will be too.

It's important to understand that the judgment these verses describe does not relate to your salvation. Christ has secured eternal life for His followers on the cross. Instead, these verses refer to a different type of judgment—one that determines your heavenly rewards. That might sound like a scary thought, but it doesn't have to be if we remember our story from above.

The two enthusiastic girls who came out first can be likened to Christians who faithfully built up God's kingdom during their lives. They will "receive a reward." On the other hand, the two visibly shaken girls who came out last correspond to Christians who were unfaithful in building up God's kingdom during their lives. They "will suffer" loss of rewards, though they "will be saved." Simply put, the way you live today will determine your rewards forever.

APPLICATION:

In 1 Corinthians 3:11–15 the apostle Paul divides everything you do in this life into one of two categories: "gold, silver, precious stones" and "wood, hay, straw." The first category refers to those things you do that have eternal significance and are done with pure motives, while the second category contains everything else. Grab a piece of paper and fold it in half. At the top of one side write, "Rewarded" and on the other side write "Burned Up." Do a quick self-review of your day yesterday, placing each activity you did on one of the two sides.

TIP:

Remember: when your time for judgment comes, it's not only what you did that will matter, but why you did those things will matter too.

UNHAPPY WITH YOUR CIRCUMSTANCES

Heading into the 1924 Paris Olympics, excitement was building throughout Europe around Scottish track star Eric Liddell. Liddell, who was one of England's premier 100-meter sprinters and who many anticipated as a gold medal favorite, had shocked the country months earlier when he decided to drop from the 100-meter race to run the 400-meter instead. This decision came after the release of the Olympic schedule, which determined the 100-meter prelims would be run on Sunday. Liddell, a devout follower of God, firmly believed he shouldn't compete on the Lord's Day and chose to remain faithful to his conviction.

As he entered the 400-meter finals, Liddell's chances of winning the gold were slim since the world record-holder was also in the race. The odds were further stacked against Liddell when he was given the outside lane, considered the worst lane on the track. Despite his predicament, Liddell left his hotel on race day with a note from his trainer stuffed in his pocket. On that note, were the encouraging words from 1 Samuel 2:30, "For those who honor me I will honor."[52]

When the time for his race finally came, Liddell found his lane and braced himself for whatever lay ahead. As the gunshot fired, Liddell started strong, later explaining his race strategy: "I ran the first 200m as quickly as I could and, with the help of God, I ran the next 200m even more strongly." Liddell broke the tape 0.8 seconds ahead of the next finisher, winning the gold medal.[53]

Liddell's story serves as an inspirational example of what it looks like to love God first, an attitude that points to the beautiful passage of Romans 8:28: "And we know that for those who love God all things work together for good, for those who are called according to his purpose." Notice that this verse does not say all things are good but that all things will work together for good.

When news broke to Liddell that his favored event was scheduled for the Sabbath day, he was put in an unfortunate situation. Ultimately remaining true to his convictions to honor God, the world-class runner focused all his training efforts heading into the games toward the 400-meter. When a poor lane position further complicated his situation, Liddell once again looked to God for strength, exemplifying what it means to look for the gold in every circumstance.

Right now God has you where you are for a reason. It can be easy to wish you were somewhere else . . . anywhere else, but that isn't where God has placed you. Although your circumstances might not seem good, God is using them for your good, and it's your job to honor Him while He does.

APPLICATION:

Decide today to look for the gold right where God has you. Every morning after waking up, make it a habit to think of one reason you're thankful to be where you are and one way you can honor God that day. It may be helpful to keep a running list by your bed of what you come up with.

TIP:

Nowhere in the Bible are believers called to deny the reality of their circumstances; rather, they are to look to God in all circumstances, regardless of what they are facing.

STAYING ON YOUR GUARD

In the intense sport of ice hockey, matches occur between two teams, each enlisting a roster full of players with various skill sets and specific roles. Of the twelve total players typically on the ice at one time, each team consists of one goalie with the singular job of protecting his or her team's goal at all costs. This turns out to be quite the task, with six competitors doing everything they can to get the puck past the goalie and into the net. Vital to the goalie's job is a full-body padded suit, including a mask, neck guard, chest protector, glove, blocker, goalie pants, jock or jill pads, skates, and a stick. With the simple yet crucial job of protecting his or her team's goal and the necessary gear to perform it, a goalie must constantly stay on his or her guard when he or she takes to the ice.

Like the role of a goalie in ice hockey, the Scriptures relate a comparable role that a Christian has when guarding his or her heart. This role is found in Proverbs 4:23: "Keep your heart with all vigilance, for from it flow the springs of life." This passage may be simple, but it teaches a lifesaving piece of wisdom.

Much as a goalie must remain focused and alert to protect his or her team's goal, you must constantly be ready for what your enemies might throw at your heart. Have no doubt: your enemies—the world, the flesh, and the devil—are doing everything they can to score on you.

Thankfully, God does not leave you exposed when it comes to guarding your heart. Similar to the way a goalie has the necessary gear to defend the goal, God has provided you with an entire Bible full of tools and instructions to help you guard your heart.

The Scripture is clear: you must protect your heart as if your life depends on it—because it does.

APPLICATION:

Take a moment to read through Proverbs 4:24–27. As you look at these verses, see if you can find six separate commands related to guarding your heart. Once you have found all six, create a bookmark for your Bible that lists these commands.

TIP:

When creating your bookmark, try rewriting each of the commands found in Proverbs 4:24–27 in a way that directly applies to your life.

PRE-COMPETITION

Kicking Off the Season 99

Maintaining a Proper Perspective 101

Riding the Bus... 103

Lacking Motivation... 105

Waiting to Compete 107

Night Before Competing 109

Facing Your Toughest Opponent..................................... 111

Feeling Pressure to Perform 113

Trash Talking.. 115

Preparing for the Postseason 117

Competing with Excellence... 119

Focusing on Christ 121

Completely Overwhelmed... 123

Your Most Important Competition 125

Competing for What Counts 127

KICKING OFF THE SEASON

The FIFA World Cup, the Lombardi Trophy, the Stanley Cup, the Larry O'Brien NBA Championship Trophy, the Wanamaker Trophy, the Wimbledon Trophy, the Commissioner's Trophy, the Harley J. Earl Trophy. These are some of the most highly treasured awards that the world of sport has to offer. Annually these trophies are presented to an elite few who, after relishing in the moment, will in most instances return the prize to a more permanent location, waiting to be grasped by the following year's winners. While these trophies are home, resting behind their glass display, countless fans will travel from around the world to get a look at these incredible prizes.

Of course, it's rather unnecessary to say that what many fans overlook when gazing at these prized possessions is what the trophies are in—a trophy case. Typically trophy cases go unnoticed, which happens to be a good thing. The purpose of a trophy case is to allow for undistracted admiration of the trophy. This concept is reasonably simple. Nevertheless, how it applies to your faith is extremely important.

To get straight to the point, as a Christian athlete you are God's trophy case. Psalm 96:8 says, "Ascribe to the LORD the glory due his name." Notice the clear message from the psalmist. As humans we're not intended to be the focus; God is. This same truth is visually expressed in Revelation 4:10–11 when John describes his heavenly vision of God's throne room: "They cast their crowns before the throne, saying, 'Worthy are you, our Lord and God, to receive glory and honor and power, for you created all things, and by your will they existed and were created.'"

Both passages point to the fact that as humans, we exist to display God's glory. Once again, to put it in sports terms, God is the trophy and you are His case.

As God's trophy case you have one purpose: to draw attention to God. Unfortunately, as a Christian there are two ways to mess this up. The first is by living in a way that the spotlight is on you. This would be comparable to a trophy case with an extravagantly carved wooden base, an intricately engraved glass design, and a lavish gold label on the bottom. The second is by living in a way disobedient to God's Word. This could be likened to a trophy case with a rotting wooden base, numerous large cracks throughout the glass, and no label at all. Both ways of living—and both trophy cases—fail at their purpose by drawing attention away from the trophy and onto the case.

Remember: as a Christian, your job is to allow for undistracted admiration of the trophy—namely, God. There's nothing you can do to make God more glorious than He already is. Your role is simply to put Him on display.

APPLICATION:

Do you have a personal mission statement? Although nowhere in the Bible are believers commanded to have one, when used in the right way a personal mission statement can serve as a great tool to remember why you do what you do. Take some time to craft your own personal mission statement. As you begin brainstorming, here are a few questions to consider:

- What is most important in my life?
- What is my purpose for living?
- What do I want others to remember about me?

TIP:

Here's an example of a personal mission statement: "My mission is to live so much like Christ that whenever my name comes up in conversation, Jesus's does too."

MAINTAINING A PROPER PERSPECTIVE

In 1976 theaters were rocked with the release of *Rocky*,[54] the first film in what would become one of the most iconic film series in history. Featuring boxer Rocky Balboa, the thirty-year span of movies (which has since been continued)[55] took fans on a dramatic ride following the legendary career of Rocky and his rise from rags to riches.[56] Within each of the six films, audiences were both awestruck and captivated by action-packed plots that came together to form one unified story. The series as a whole can be encapsulated in one of the most recognizable scenes from *Rocky II*.

Having fought a brutal rematch against reigning champion Apollo Creed, Rocky in the final round delivers crushing blows to knock down the champion and claim victory for himself.[57] Bruised and battered by the fight, Rocky is called on to give a post-match speech. With blood and sweat dripping down his face, Rocky struggled between breaths to get his words out. In a final charge directed at his wife, Rocky lifted high his championship belt and exclaimed, "Yo, Adrian! I did it!"[58]

This scene perfectly captures the stereotypical end to most inspirational movies. It's a storyline that sells tickets and carries the undertone of an even greater story with an even greater hero. The story is life, and the hero is Jesus. Let's take a peek at Philippians 2:6–11, which explains that Jesus . . .

> who, though he was in the form of God, did not count equality with God a thing to be grasped, but emptied himself, by taking the form of a servant, being born in the likeness of men. And being found in human form, he humbled himself by becoming obedient to the point of death, even death on a cross. Therefore God has highly exalted

him and bestowed on him the name that is above every name, so that at the name of Jesus every knee should bow, in heaven and on earth and under the earth, and every tongue confess that Jesus Christ is Lord, to the glory of God the Father.

The reality these verses teach is that all of human HIS-tory has one hero, and His name is Jesus. That's why as Christians we must be careful.

It can be easy to watch a movie like *Rocky II* and envision your life as a story in which you are the hero, not Jesus. As we have seen from Philippians, this perspective would be entirely wrong. The message the Bible conveys is that your story is part of a bigger story—a story that focuses on Jesus. In terms of a movie, you might consider your life as if you were in a supporting role in a film that already has the main character. To say it another way, God has put Jesus on center stage and your role is to keep the spotlight on Him.

APPLICATION:

When film producers create movies, they typically follow what is called a plot diagram. A plot diagram consists of six major areas of emphasis that come together to form a compelling story. Those six areas are 1. Exposition (introduction) 2. Conflict (problem) 3. Rising Action 4. Climax (resolution to the conflict) 5. Falling Action, and 6. Resolution (ending). With what you've learned in mind, create your own plot diagram covering the story of human HIS-tory. Do your best to assign specific historical events to each category of your diagram.

TIP:

Here are a few chapters from the Bible that will help assist you as you create your plot diagram: Genesis 1–3; Matthew 26–28; and Revelation 21–22.

RIDING THE BUS

The Greensborough High girls volleyball team had finally finished loading the bus when the coach stood up and started her usual instructions.

"All right, ladies—did you make sure and grab everything you need?" With a few heads nodding and the words "Yes, coach," echoing throughout the bus, the coach looked down at her clipboard. "Make sure you have both knee pads, your water bottle, uniform, and shoes." As she rolled through the checklist, the girls opened their bags to double-check that they had everything they needed for the matches that evening. After reaching the end of her list, the coach paused and then made her usual final comment. "Remember, ladies—if you don't have your gear tonight, you won't be playing." The coach smiled at her team, and the bus ride started.

Having the proper equipment is a must for any athlete who wants to be able to compete in his or her sport. This story serves as a reminder of that fact. Interestingly, the same concept is true for your faith. Thankfully, Ephesians 6:13–17 tells you precisely what you need.

> *Therefore take up the whole armor of God, that you may be able to withstand in the evil day, and having done all, to stand firm. Stand therefore, having fastened on the belt of truth, and having put on the breastplate of righteousness, and, as shoes for your feet, having put on the readiness given by the gospel of peace. In all circumstances take up the shield of faith, with which you can extinguish all the flaming darts of the evil one; and take the helmet of salvation, and the sword of the Spirit, which is the word of God.*

Wow! Now that's a checklist. Let's take a moment to explore what each of these means:

- The "belt of truth" is what keeps your life from falling apart. It's the idea of truthfulness inside and out—a person who holds to what God says is true without hypocrisy.
- The "breastplate of righteousness" is what protects you when the enemy tries to shake you at your core. This is not your fluctuating righteousness, but Christ's perfect righteousness.
- The "shoes for your feet" is the gospel, and it's your firm foundation. Keeping the gospel fresh in your mind is what keeps you from slipping spiritually.
- The "shield of faith" is what stops the enemy's attacks before they can have an effect. It's more than head knowledge; it's heartfelt trust in Who God is and what God has said.
- The "helmet of salvation" is one of the most vital pieces of protection from the damaging assaults of the adversary. This is mentally dwelling on your salvation in Christ and the positive blessings salvation brings.
- The "sword of the Spirit, which is the word of God," is your method of attack. The Word of God is how you go on offense.

APPLICATION:

There you have the complete checklist. How have you been doing when it comes to wearing your spiritual equipment? Whether you've been doing great or not so great, tomorrow morning give it a shot. Mentally rehearse putting on each piece of spiritual equipment before you get out of bed.

TIP:

Draw each of the six pieces of spiritual armor on individual flashcards to serve as a creative reminder of the spiritual gear you should be putting on daily.

LACKING MOTIVATION

It was the evening of August 12, 2000, and the atmosphere at the Indianapolis Natatorium pool was electric. Fans watched in awe as the 200-meter butterfly Olympic trial finals drew to a close. At the final turn, fifteen-year-old Michael Phelps was in fourth place, just out of qualification for the United States Olympic team. The NBC broadcasters, who had much to say about the youngster's age, expressed their excitement.

"What a race right now for second! Here comes Phelps up in lane number five!"[59] The crowd roared as the final few meters rushed by, and Phelps made one final push to the end. With the touch of his fingers on the wall, the race was complete and countless eyes turned to the natatorium scoreboard to see who had qualified. Moments later, the results were in. Phelps had done it. Finishing second secured the high-school sophomore's ticket to the 2000 Olympics and made him the youngest Olympic swimming qualifier in 68 years.[60] When describing the moment to an interviewer, Phelps's sister put to words the emotions many felt: "I was so psyched . . . Michael is incredible."[61]

It's moments like this that can inspire humanity to greater heights. Following Phelps's success, swimmers across the nation were able to put on their suits with a new sense of purpose and confidence. With Phelps in their minds, they were free to imagine that they could do more than they ever thought possible.

As we consider the powerful motivation that Phelps's Olympic qualifying performance aroused in the hearts of many, let's compare Titus 2:11–14 to see how this story relates to your faith. The passage says, "For the grace of God has appeared, bringing salvation for all people, training us to renounce ungodliness and worldly passions, and to live self-controlled, upright, and godly lives in the present age, waiting for our blessed hope, the appearing of the glory of our great

God and Savior Jesus Christ, who gave himself for us to redeem us from all lawlessness and to purify for himself a people for his own possession who are zealous for good works."

Notice specifically the motivation that the final verse of this passage relays. It says that "[Christ] gave himself for . . ." Anytime we read in the Scriptures a reason Christ died, it deserves our full attention. The verse then continues with two reasons for Christ's death. One, Christ died "to redeem [Christians]" from lawlessness; and two, to purify for Himself a people who are eager "for good works." The first leads to the second. In essence, Christ's death for you, should inspire good works from you through the Holy Spirit in you. Let's draw this back to our story of Phelps.

If a fifteen-year-old qualifying for his first Olympics was enough to stir up the hearts of a nation full of swimmers, how much more should Jesus's death stir up your heart?

APPLICATION:

Next time you have a break in the action, search "Michael Phelps Qualifies for First Olympics" online and watch the full video of Michael's inspirational swim. Once you've finished, take some time to reflect on all that Christ's death truly means and how that moment has the power to inspire a lifetime's worth of motivation.

TIP:

The original video of Michael's incredible swim can be found on the NBC Sports website or NBC Sports YouTube channel.

WAITING TO COMPETE

"Next, please."

The long line of hungry parents and fans slowly made their way closer to the concessions stand as Jackson, a twelve-year-old boy, stepped to the counter.

"Um, yes. I would like one nacho, a popcorn, and a Twix." Jackson paused as he squinted at the menu. "Oh, yeah, and a Dr. Pepper, please." Each of the young boy's requests was gently echoed behind the counter as the group of workers gathered the items.

"Will that be all?" asked the girl taking Jackson's order. The twelve-year-old quickly scanned the display of products behind the counter before he added, "Actually, could I also have two Laffy Taffy?"

"Sure," responded the girl, gently handing the items across the counter.

With his items in hand, Jackson made his way to the cashier's table, where he dumped his armful of goodies in front of the uninterested worker.

"Your total will be $9.50. Would you like to buy a raffle ticket?"

Before the young boy could respond, his face flushed red, and heat waves began to course through his body. Reaching into his pocket, Jackson fumbled through his money and began to count out loud, "Five. Six. Seven. Seven-fifty. Seven-fifty-one. Seven-fifty-two." Jackson paused and quickly returned his hand to his pocket, shuffling around. The sound of a crinkling gum wrapper was all he heard. Returning his empty hand to the counter, the young boy stood silently.

Unmoved by the situation, the blank-faced worker stated the obvious. "I'm sorry, young man, but you don't have enough to buy all of this."

The disappointed boy slowly turned around, deep in thought, deciding which items he would return.

This story presents a humiliating situation for anyone to be in, one that Jackson could have easily avoided if he would have counted the cost—a principle that happens to be quite biblical.

To understand this principle from a biblical perspective, let's look at a parable found in Luke 14:28–30, 33. In this parable Jesus said, "For which of you, desiring to build a tower, does not first sit down and count the cost, whether he has enough to complete it? Otherwise, when he has laid a foundation and is not able to finish, all who see it begin to mock him, saying, 'This man began to build and was not able to finish.' . . . So therefore, any one of you who does not renounce all that he has cannot be my disciple." The message from these verses is clear: following Jesus comes at a cost.

Unfortunately, all too many people treat Jesus as Jackson did at the concession stand. They want to pick and choose the various blessings that Jesus brings, but they don't count the cost of following Him. The reality is that we live in a world that likes to think that following Jesus is as easy as 1–2–3. They want a costless Christianity, but that is not what Christ offers. Following Christ comes at a cost; Jesus said it Himself.

APPLICATION:

Check out Jesus's words in Matthew 10:34–39, which give further clarity on this subject. Pay special attention to verse 39 and see if you can find an answer to the question "What does Jesus ask of those who follow Him?"

TIP:

If you find yourself discouraged after counting the cost of following Jesus, remember the great cost that Jesus paid to save you.

NIGHT BEFORE COMPETING

*B**uzz! Buzz! Buzz!***
The basketball buzzer signaled three minutes until game time and both teams had taken the court. That is, except for one player. Stacey, a varsity starter, was nervously pacing back and forth in the home team locker room. After a few trips between the tightly packed walls, Stacey began to mumble to herself. "I can't play without them. I have no option. I have to wait." As her face continued to turn brighter shades of red, Stacey anxiously checked her phone to see if she had any new messages. Then she continued her rant. "Come on, Mom. I . . ."

Before Stacey could get the words out of her mouth, the squeaking sound of the locker room door interrupted her frustrations. Stacey's mom walked into the locker room and stood at a distance, dangling a pair of bright red, white, and blue Superman socks. "Here you go," she said with a wink. "Now you can't lose."

It may come as no surprise that in the world of competitive athletics, there are countless "Staceys" out there, holding hard and fast to some superstitious item or pregame ritual they credit for helping them perform at their best. You might even have your own special something that you wear or do before competitions. But what might be a little more unexpected is that in a certain respect God does too. We find out about this in 2 Timothy 2:20–21: "Now in a great house there are not only vessels of gold and silver but also of wood and clay, some for honorable use, some for dishonorable. Therefore, if anyone cleanses himself from what is dishonorable, he will be a vessel for honorable use, set apart as holy, useful to the master of the house, ready for every good work."

Although God is not superstitious, these verses make clear that He does set apart specific people for special purposes. Of course, after learning about this extraordinary reality, the next logical question for many Christians will be "How can I be one of those people?" That's where context comes into play. If you go back up to 2 Timothy 2:19, we learn the answer: "But God's firm foundation stands, bearing this seal: 'The Lord knows those who are his,' and, 'Let everyone who names the name of the Lord depart from iniquity.'" Fleeing from sin results in being set apart by God for special purposes.

Like Stacey, you might have something special that you bring out for important occasions. Well, so does God. Would you like to be used by God in that way? You can, by "[departing] from iniquity."

APPLICATION:

An initial step in fleeing from sin is knowing what sin you need to flee from in the first place. If God were to look at your life, what is one area you believe might prevent Him from using you for special purposes? Although it may feel uncomfortable, ask God for help to see any areas of your life that are not in line with His Word. You can begin by praying Psalm 139:23–24: "Search me, O God, and know my heart! Try me and know my thoughts! And see if there be any grievous way in me, and lead me in the way everlasting!"

TIP:

Though it may be tempting to skip prayer in favor of trying to find personal faults on your own, prayer is an essential step in seeing sins that you would otherwise be blind to.

FACING YOUR TOUGHEST OPPONENT

Philippians 4:13 is one of the most popular Bible verses used among athletes. You can find it labeled on duffel bags, eye black, water bottles, and about any other piece of athletic merchandise you can think of. For anyone who's read the verse, there's no mystery for why it's popular. Who doesn't want to hear, "I can do all things through him who strengthens me"? What an encouraging piece of Scripture!

But today it's time you learn two other verses that are essential for correctly understanding the popular Philippians 4:13 passage—two verses that come directly before it. Introducing Philippians 4:11–12, which says, "Not that I am speaking of being in need, for I have learned in whatever situation I am to be content. I know how to be brought low, and I know how to abound. In any and every circumstance, I have learned the secret of facing plenty and hunger, abundance and need." It's only after those words that Paul says, "I can do all things through him who strengthens me."

Paul wasn't writing a motivational quote to inspire athletes. He was sharing the secret behind contentment in every situation. Unfortunately, that's where this verse is commonly misunderstood. Most often, athletes quote this verse as encouragement against insurmountable odds. They believe it means they can do the impossible. Although that may sound exciting, hopefully you've realized that's not what the verse is saying. This verse is promising so much more.

For athletes, the real meaning behind this verse is that no matter whether you win or lose, no matter if you're the champion of the world or the last-place finisher, in whatever circumstance your sport brings, Christ provides you with the strength to be content.

APPLICATION:

As you gear up for your next competition, pick a friend, team-mate, or coach to share what you learned about Philippians 4:13. Explain the passage's context and how understanding the previous verses might change how someone understands the verse. Conclude by offering the encouragement that when used in its proper context, Philippians 4:13 makes a tremendous promise for believers: contentment is always possible.

TIP:

If you hear a fellow Christian athlete using the Philippians 4:13 verse out of context, you may be tempted to correct his or her error. In such a case it would be wise to wait until you and the culprit are alone before graciously informing them of a proper understanding of the verse. (You will also want to make sure you are personally modeling contentment in Christ in your own life.)

FEELING PRESSURE TO PERFORM

In preparations for her fifth and final Olympics at Tokyo in 2021, American beach volleyball player Kerri Walsh Jennings said this to the *Los Angeles Times* about her mindset going into the games: "You can want something too much and suffocate it. . . . So now [it's such a] perception switch. There is just so much stuff bigger than [Olympic volleyball], even though this is huge to us. It's our careers, it's our lives, it's our passion . . . however, we will now see it with more gratitude, and I believe less stress, which will allow us to play better."[62]

It's evident from her words that Walsh Jennings was on to something. When an athlete's focus is placed on the wrong thing, it not only causes problems internally but also acts as a performance de-enhancer. So consider this devotion a "perception switch." Although this change might push you, it's worth giving some real thought to what's next. We'll begin by considering something "bigger than" competition. In fact, it's the biggest thing you can remember as a Christian athlete and it happens to be a story.

The story starts in Isaiah 43:7, where God says that He "created [you] for [His] glory, [and that He] formed and made [you]." When God created you, it was not because He had to but because He wanted you to enjoy and glorify Him. Heartbreakingly, instead of returning love toward God, Isaiah 53:6 begins by saying, "All we like sheep have gone astray; we have turned—every one—to his own way." All people, including you, have rejected the God Who made and loves us. To put it in less elegant terms, we've spit in God's face and walked away. Yet God did the unthinkable. Isaiah 53:6 goes on to say that God sent His own Son "And the LORD has laid on him the iniquity of us all." God the Father crushed God the Son to pave the way for you and every other rebel to have a perfectly restored relationship with Himself so that you might enjoy and glorify Him once again. If you're a Christian, that's your story.

You don't have to wait any longer to reach the conclusion that Walsh Jennings shared. Right now, wherever you find yourself, come to grips with the reality there's something so much bigger than sports. Yes, this is entirely different from what the world teaches, and that's okay. You weren't created to be an athlete but to enjoy and glorify God forever.

APPLICATION:

Think ahead a few years to what life will look like when your days as an athlete are finished. Maybe you envision yourself going on to compete collegiately or even professionally. Great! Think even further until you reach the end when you can't play sports any longer. Now ask your future self these two questions:

1. Who am I?
2. Why am I here?

TIP:

If your heart is set on Christ, your answer to the two questions above will never change.

TRASH TALKING

It was late Saturday morning in the Richmond School District, and countless tired teenagers were turning over in bed to grab their phones and begin the day. As social feeds were updated and scrolling began, it became evident that a social media firestorm had gone down the night before, following the game.

To start the battle, BB_Baller_Jackson, one of Richmond's players, took it upon himself to share his thoughts after the game: "Sorry we had to blow #1 ranked St. Francis out of the water last night. What a game!"

Yolo_Ridder, a player from St. Francis, quickly responded. "@BB_Baller_Jackson, I wouldn't call a 4-point win a blowout. Besides, I'm sure it would have felt better if you were able to get in the game last night."

BB_Baller_Jackson shot back, "Number of minutes played doesn't matter, numbers on the score board do. Nice try."

BallerMama89 added her input. "@BB_Baller_Jackson, don't even get me started on last night's game. My son was putting up points all game. Plus, his uniform was classy. In my book, that's a win."

The scene here presents us with three separate characters making three different errors, each of which will hopefully become clear as we examine an appropriate passage of Scripture.

Ephesians 4:29 includes the following command given to believers regarding their speech. "Let no corrupting talk come out of your mouths, but only such as is good for building up, as fits the occasion, that it may give grace to those who hear." Packed within this single sentence is a powerful test you can use to gauge whether you should say something. You can think of it in three simple questions:

1. Is what I'm about to say honorable to God?

2. Is what I'm about to say helpful to others?

3. Is what I'm about to say necessary to the conversation?

To summarize: Is it honorable? Is it helpful? Is it necessary?

Given what we've learned, let's take a moment to break down the social media episode from earlier to see how things stack up:

- @BB_Baller_Jackson's words were not "honorable." He lied when he called a 4-point win a blowout and was unkind with his remarks towards Yolo_Ridder.

- @Yolo_Ridder's words were not "helpful." Drawing attention to the fact that BB_Baller_Jackson didn't play was not beneficial to the conversation.

- @BallerMama89's words were not "necessary." She clearly didn't need to offer her input into the situation.

At this point you might be left scratching your head thinking, "What's left to say then?" Great question! When you put into practice Ephesians 4:29, you're left only saying things that "give grace to those who hear."

APPLICATION:

How would you do if someone followed you around for a full day and graded your words based on the three questions listed above? Make the necessary changes to the words coming out of your mouth. As you do, remember the questions "Is it honorable? Is it helpful? Is it necessary?" as a quick reference guide when making conversational choices.

TIP:

Do you want an even better way to remember the three questions above? Try memorizing Ephesians 4:29.

PREPARING FOR THE POSTSEASON

During the 1998 FIFA World Cup, Brazil faced off against France.[63] Twenty-seven minutes into the match, France's Emmanuel Petit sent a corner kick flying through the air as attacking midfielder Zinedine Zidane forcefully headed the ball straight into the back of the net for a goal, giving France a 1–0 lead.[64] In the spur of the moment, French team manager Aimé Jacquet[65] rushed onto the field, stopping the game. With a stadium full of curious onlookers, Jacquet awarded Zidane a shining gold medal and organized the players in a parade behind the midfielder. Stunned, the crowd continued to watch as Jacquet threw confetti into the air, marching his team across the field in celebration of Zidane's goal.

This moment might have gone down as one of the most unusual incidents in sports history, if it really happened. In reality, it's only partially true. Everything up to the point of Zidane's goal did occur in the 1998 FIFA World Cup. However, Jacquet's strange celebration did not, and there's a reason for that. The point of soccer is to score goals, and there's a point to this exaggerated story too. In the Gospel of Luke, Jesus offers a parable that falls right in line with the lesson that this inflated story teaches. It's found in Luke 17:7–10.

> *Will any one of you who has a servant plowing or keeping sheep say to him when he has come in from the field, "Come at once and recline at table"? Will he not rather say to him, "Prepare supper for me, and dress properly, and serve me while I eat and drink, and afterward you will eat and drink"? Does he thank the servant because he did what was commanded? So you also, when you have done all that you were commanded, say, "We are unworthy servants; we have only done what was our duty."*

In this Scripture passage Jesus draws a meaningful connection we can relate to the world of sports. Like Zidane, when a soccer player scores a goal, they have succeeded in their objective. They shouldn't expect a medal or parade; they were only doing their job. Similarly, as a Christian, when you serve God you shouldn't expect health, wealth, and prosperity; you're simply doing your job. That isn't to say that God doesn't bless His servants. Psalm 5:12 says, "For you bless the righteous, O Lord." But that doesn't mean God has to.

A great example of where this erroneous thinking might come into play for a Christian athlete is in preparation for a competition. It's not unusual to see followers of Christ act on their best behavior leading up to an important competition in the hopes that God will bless them with success. Unfortunately, this is the flawed mindset that Jesus was getting at.

If you're a follower of Christ, God has already given you the greatest blessing you could receive: Christ Himself. Now that you've received the gift of salvation, your service for God should spring from gratitude for what God has already done, not a desire to somehow manipulate God into blessing you. Christians serve Christ. That's the point.

APPLICATION:

If you notice yourself changing your behavior leading into an important competition with the hopes of earning God's blessing, take note. The areas where you are acting differently likely should receive your greatest attention and effort toward improving on a regular basis.

TIP:

God often chooses to bless His servants' labors simply because of Who He is, a good God, not because He has to.

COMPETING WITH EXCELLENCE

Ask any devoted Los Angeles Lakers fan what the number 24 represents, and he or she will immediately tell you, Kobe Bryant. Throughout his career, Bryant not only marked himself as one of the most skilled players on the court but also transformed the NBA through his incredible work ethic.[66] Bryant's work ethic was so distinct from the typical standard that it earned the title "Mamba Mentality." In his book, *Relentless*, Bryant's trainer summarized the "Mamba" mindset in this way: "That's Kobe: everything he does is all about excellence. Everything."[67]

The words of Bryant's trainer provide a fitting description of the type of mindset that should define every follower of Christ—one that finds its roots in the life of the Savior.

In Mark 7:31–37 we find a story of a crowd flocking to Jesus. As this crowd approached, they brought to Jesus a man who was deaf and mute, wanting Christ to cure him. Jesus responded to the crowd's request by bringing the man aside and healing him. When the crowd saw what Jesus had done, verse 37 records their reaction: "And they were astonished beyond measure, saying, 'He has done all things well. He even makes the deaf hear and the mute speak.'"

This is the standard Christ has left His followers with, to do "all things well." Sounds impossible, right? Thankfully it's not. 1 John 2:5–6 shares how you can live up to this calling: "By this we may know that we are in him: whoever says he abides in him ought to walk in the same way in which he walked." Christ in you gives you that ability to live as He did in this world. Excellence in your life is a reflection of Christ in your heart.

In a world of half-hearted efforts, doing the bare minimum, and striving to slide by, Bryant looked different in his approach to basketball. As a follower of Christ, you should look different in your approach to life. Christ expects you to demonstrate an attitude of excellence in all areas of your life, and rightfully so. You have the greatest demonstration of excellent living in Christ Himself, and right alongside that, you have Christ's power to propel you to live up to that standard.

If you want to look different, compete with excellence. If you want to look like Christ, do everything with excellence.

APPLICATION:

Having a mindset that goes above and beyond is something that may take some time to develop, but you can begin right away. Starting now, strive for excellence in everything you do. If you're doing homework, do it with excellence. Filling water bottles? Go above and beyond. Washing the dishes? Raise the bar. What excellence looks like in your life depends on the circumstances that God has placed you in, but the mindset remains the same.

TIP:

Excellence does not equal speed. Applying care and conscientiousness are two important components of living excellently.

FOCUSING ON CHRIST

Most people inducted into a hall of fame make it because they spent their lives pursuing and accomplishing something great. There's a hall of fame for football, basketball, baseball, and many other sports. Even the Scriptures contain a type of hall of fame. It's found in Hebrews chapter 11—a section of Scripture highlighting some of the most well-known characters in the Bible. Many have titled this chapter the Hall of Faith, which is a fitting label.

What makes the Bible's Hall of Faith so unique is that it emphasizes its inductees for a different reason than most other halls of fames. Despite the fact that it contains figures like Enoch, Noah, and Abraham, the Hall of Faith chapter ends with a curious set of verses in Hebrews 11:39–40: "And all these, though commended through their faith, did not receive what was promised, since God had provided something better for us, that apart from us they should not be made perfect." To make clear, these were considered some of the greatest Bible characters of all time. Yet these verses express that their distinguishing mark was they didn't receive what was promised. What does that mean? And why is it a good thing? The answer to these questions is found earlier in the chapter in Hebrews 11:13–16.

> *These all died in faith, not having received the things promised, but having seen them and greeted them from afar, and having acknowledged that they were strangers and exiles on the earth. For people who speak thus make it clear that they are seeking a homeland. If they had been thinking of that land from which they had gone out, they would have had opportunity to return. But as it is, they desire a better country, that is, a heavenly one. Therefore God is not ashamed to be called their God, for he has prepared for them a city.*

The point that Hebrews 11 is drawing out is that each of these Hall of Faith figures was fixing his or her eyes on the promises of God, not on accomplishing great things. The amazing accomplishments that they're known for were simply a result of their faith, not the focus of their faith. Choosing to live their lives with a focus on God and heaven, these Hall of Faithers were willing to do whatever God asked of them.

That's where the Hall of Faith differs from what most people would expect. Unlike typical halls of fames, the Hall of Faith highlights its inductees more for their focus on God and less for their accomplishments. This is where the Hall of Faith applies to you. If you set your focus on making a great name for yourself, you might be disappointed because God's plans can be different than yours. But if you focus on God and His promises, you can be confident that God can use you for more than you would ever imagine.

APPLICATION:

Find a time to read through Hebrews 11, noting the various Bible figures found within. Once you've finished, pick one or two characters from the list to think about. (You may need to reread their stories to refresh your memory.) Specifically consider how God was the focus of your chosen characters' lives and not their great accomplishments.

TIP:

As an example from above, consider the story of Noah. Having been warned by God of a coming global flood, Noah obediently built an ark and was used by God to save a remnant of humanity from the catastrophe. His world-changing accomplishment was clearly one of faith, and likely not something he had always dreamed of doing.

COMPLETELY OVERWHELMED

The shadowy figure of two female high schoolers could be dimly traced, sitting on the small cold concrete steps outside the school gymnasium. Faintly visible by a flickering streetlight were tear marks staining the faces of both girls. The younger of the two sat with her knees pulled in tight and her arms wrapped around her body, nervously rocking back and forth. The other remained close with a piece of paper in her hand. The roster for the girls basketball team had been posted that evening and it was clear that the younger of the two girls didn't make the cut.

Glancing at the paper, the older girl carefully placed her arms around the younger one and whispered, "It will be all right. God will never give you more than you can handle."

This story is a heartwarming example of what true friendship looks like. Sadly, the touching scene is tainted by a subtle lie that can mislead Christians. The lie is found in the words "God will never give you more than you can handle." This common phrase happens to be a misunderstanding of God's promise found in 1 Corinthians 10:13, which teaches that God will never allow you to be tempted beyond your ability to endure. If truth be told, God will give you more than you can handle, and the Bible says so.

We discover this hard truth in 2 Corinthians 1:8–10 when Paul says, "For we do not want you to be unaware, brothers, of the affliction we experienced in Asia. For we were so utterly burdened beyond our strength that we despaired of life itself. Indeed, we felt that we had received the sentence of death. But that was to make us rely not on ourselves but on God who raises the dead. He delivered us from such a deadly peril, and he will deliver us. On him we have set our hope that he will deliver us again."

Notice Paul's exact words. "We were so utterly burdened beyond our strength." To say it another way, Paul and his fellow workers had been given more than they could handle. Yet Paul's thought continues, "But that was to make us rely not on ourselves but on God." Within these final words lies the key to unlocking the lie mentioned in our story for a much greater truth. God will give you more than you can handle, but He will never give you more than He can handle. His reasoning? That you will depend on Him.

Thinking back to our story from above, the two girls shared a disheartening time. Unfortunately, the older friend's comment is similar to the one that many innocent Christians can also make without realizing their error. The deception in these falsely reassuring words can be extremely harmful when it encourages Christians to rely on their own strength in overwhelming times. God will push you past your limits. Yes, that can be a hard pill to swallow, but He does this so you will come to the end of yourself and begin to rely on Him.

APPLICATION:

Are you overwhelmed? God likely has you exactly where He wants you. But what do you do when you don't know what to do? You follow in the footsteps of the Savior: pray. In the garden of Gethsemane Jesus prepared to face the most overwhelming task of all, bearing the wrath of God on the cross. How did He respond? Jesus "fell on his face and prayed" (Matthew 26:39), forever leaving His followers an example to follow. It might not be glamorous, and it might not be flashy, but it is really that simple. Fall on your face and pray.

TIP:

You may find it helpful to reread the account of Jesus in the garden of Gethsemane as you prepare to enter into prayer with your heavenly Father. You can find the account in Matthew 26:36–46.

YOUR MOST IMPORTANT COMPETITION

Standing atop the Olympic halfpipe, American snowboarder Chloe Kim had one of the most extraordinary sensations an athlete can ever experience. She was preparing for her final run in the 2022 Beijing Olympics, having the gold medal already secured. With an initial run scoring a mark that would remain unbeaten for the rest of the competition, Kim now had the opportunity at one last victory run.[68] With no pressure weighing her down, the American snowboarder was able to compete with the complete freedom of knowing she was already victorious. Kim's experience embodies a freedom with which few athletes will ever have the privilege of competing—that is, unless you're a Christian.

As a Christian, you are able to compete in a way that a non-Christian doesn't. The difference is explained in 1 Corinthians 15:57: "But thanks be to God, who gives us the victory through our Lord Jesus Christ." At the heart of this verse is the reminder that because of Christ's death on the cross, you've already won. This truth offers a breath of fresh air in a world that is working tirelessly to achieve something that can only be received. Who wants the burden of living up to expectations that have been placed on them? As a Christian, you don't have to. Instead, you can compete *from* victory instead of *for* it.

This is what it means to compete as a Christian athlete. When you recognize that you've already won, you have complete freedom to compete like Kim in her final victory run. Regardless of the outcome of your competition, you're already victorious.

APPLICATION:

As you prepare for your next competition, write the word *victorious* on something you will see before competing. Use the word as a reminder to set your focus on the victory Christ has already brought you. Then—compete victoriously.

TIP:

Not sure where to write the word *victorious*? Try putting it on a sticky note inside your shoes for a reminder when you lace up.

COMPETING FOR WHAT COUNTS

They call it the *Statue of a Victorious Youth*. Proudly on display in the Getty Villa Museum in southern California, the life-size statue captures the figure of a youth athlete crowning himself with an olive wreath.[69] Assumed by scholars to be a victor's statue, the bronze casting would have originally memorialized a winner of the ancient Olympic Games. Now, nearly two millennia later, the statue has lost its luster, missing both feet, eyes, and the original colors.[70] It serves as a stark reminder about how temporary fame can be—a topic clearly spoken of in Scripture.

In Isaiah 40:6–8 the Lord God made a bold declaration about the fleeting nature of fame:

"A voice says, 'Cry!' And I said, 'What shall I cry?' All flesh is grass, and all its beauty is like the flower of the field. The grass withers, the flower fades when the breath of the LORD blows on it; surely the people are grass. The grass withers, the flower fades, but the word of our God will stand forever."

As these verses indicate, if your desire is to live for something that will last forever, then fame is not your thing. What does that leave you to choose from? Building on the words of Isaiah, 1 Peter 1:23–25 gives us some insight:

"Since you have been born again, not of perishable seed but of imperishable, through the living and abiding word of God; for 'All flesh is like grass and all its glory like the flower of grass. The grass withers, and the flower falls, but the word of the Lord remains forever.' And this word is the good news that was preached to you."

To live for what counts is to live for the "word of God," and as the above verses explain, the "word of God" is the message of Jesus Christ—that is, everything Jesus lived and taught. Peter clarified this in verse 25, saying that the "word of the Lord" was the "good news" that was preached to you.

Let's briefly think back to the *Statue of a Victorious Youth*. In its prime, the statue would have represented all the fame an athlete could dream of. It symbolized prestige, heroism, and admiration by the masses. Now the statue of honor sits decayed and broken as a museum artifact. The lesson is simple: if you want to live a life that counts and you're looking for fame to do that, then you're looking in the wrong place. In the Scriptures God has clearly spelled out that living a life that counts is centered on the message of Jesus Christ. Which raises the question—what are you living for?

APPLICATION:

Ask a parent or coach if he or she can recall who the most famous sports figure was when he or she was growing up and see if you recognize the name. To take things a step further, ask your parent or coach to highlight some of the sports figure's most notable accomplishments.

TIP:

Do a quick online search for the sports figure your parent or coach shared with you and see what information you can find.

POST-COMPETITION

Fell Short of Winning...131

Knowing What to Say...133

Battling Pride 135

Won an Upset 137

The Morning After Competing..............................139

A Record was Broken 141

Assessing Your Actions...143

Conquering Envy...145

Frustrated with the Season....................................147

After a Hard Loss..149

Responding to Adversity 151

Silencing Comparison...153

Confessing Sin 155

Came Down to the Wire 157

Encountering Crisis...159

Made a Big Mistake...161

Responding to Praise 163

Disheartened by Defeat 165

Things Aren't Going Your Way 167

Following a Poor Performance 169

Finished with High School Sports 171

FELL SHORT OF WINNING

One summer three swimmers attempted to swim the 650 miles across Hudson Bay. To most people that sounds crazy, but to each of these swimmers it was a challenge they thought they could handle. The first to try was twenty-three-year-old Brad Daily, a novice swimmer with a big ego. On an early June morning, Daily jumped into Hudson Bay with a boat crew at his side. After two and a half long hours of struggling through the frigid water, Daily started to drown, and his team was forced to pull him into the boat.

It wasn't too long after Daily's attempt until word got out that another swimmer would make a go at the feat. Motivated partially by Daily's failure and partly by his background in triathlons, forty-six-year-old Jimmy Davis decided to give the challenge a try. Unlike Daily, Davis put his experience from triathlons to use. Having carefully planned all the details for the big day, on a late July morning Davis went to work. Hour after hour ticked by until an outstanding seven hours later, when Davis's fatigue got the best of him and he was forced to stop. Like Daily, Davis had failed.

With two swimmers down, most people thought that would be the end of the attempts to cross the Hudson Bay, but nearly two months after Davis's failure, a retired Olympic world champion named Lorenzo Diaz made a surprise announcement. He had been training, and he was going to try swimming across Hudson Bay. The difference in Diaz's attempt was that everything would be set up perfectly. There would be a film crew following, a world-record adjudicator verifying, and a boat crew providing for all of Diaz's special needs. On the big day, everything came together perfectly. The water was smooth, and the outside temperature was ideal for the swim. At the sound of a horn, on the pristine September morning Diaz dove into the water at 6:00 a.m. sharp. Then he swam and swam and swam. A grueling eighteen hours and ten minutes later, Diaz finally stopped. Unfortunately, he hadn't reached the end, falling short of his goal. Later, when asked about the attempt, he simply explained, "My legs stopped working, and that was the end of it."

At this point you might be wondering how far each of the swimmers made it. Here are the numbers: Daily made it 3.28 miles, Davis made it 13.03 miles, and Diaz made it 139.80 miles. Let's back up. Do you remember how wide the Hudson Bay is? 650 miles. None of the swimmers were even close to swimming the entire distance.

So what's the point of this story? Trying to swim the Hudson Bay is like trying to earn your salvation through good works. Ephesians 2:8–9 says, "For by grace you have been saved through faith. And this is not your own doing; it is the gift of God, not a result of works, so that no one may boast." The life-changing, awe-inspiring good news that these verses offer is that salvation is through faith alone, not works.

Much like the three swimmers from our story, if you try to earn your salvation, you will fall far short of your goal, no matter who you are or how hard you try. Thankfully, no part of your salvation is earned; it is a gift, and that's what's amazing about salvation: you can't earn it, but you can receive it.

APPLICATION:

Find a quiet place this evening to sit and think about the good news that salvation is a gift. Try answering these questions: "What would my life look like if I had to earn my salvation?" and "What did my salvation cost Christ?"

TIP:

As you ponder the gift of salvation, here are a few verses to consider: 1 Corinthians 6:20; Matthew 26:28; and Isaiah 53:4–6.

KNOWING WHAT TO SAY

The following words come directly from a sermon that a Russian pastor gave while preaching to a church in America:

> I grew up in Siberia where it's all about [Greco-Roman] wrestling . . . and one brother from our church . . . he grew up in a Christian home, he was a really good wrestler, and I said to him when he became a champion of our region, I said, "You know it would be great for you to talk with kids to share good news." And he said, "You know I'm very, very busy. I'm just preparing for national championship. After becoming champion of Russia, I will be willing to do that." So he became a champion of Russia, and I said, "Great! It's time for you to minister for the Lord." And he said, "You know, I'm really busy. I'm just preparing for Europe." And he became European [champion], and he was about to become a world champion. And he was practicing in Italy, and all these young people, they love to drive crazy in Ferrari car. So he was driving with his friends and got into a car accident. And he lost his legs. He could not anymore walk himself. And when he's witnessing now and telling his story, he's sometimes crying [because] he had a great opportunity to minister for the Lord with his legs, but he lost it.[71]

This story is a tragedy, not only because the wrestler lost his legs but even more so because he lost a wonderful opportunity to minister for the Lord. Sadly, this missed opportunity could have been easily avoided if the Siberian wrestler had taken the words of James 4:13–14 to heart: "Come now, you who say, 'Today or tomorrow we will go into such and such a town and spend a year there and trade and make a profit'— yet you do not know what tomorrow will bring. What is your life? For you are a mist that appears for a little time and then vanishes." The message of this passage is clear: life is short, and tomorrow is never guaranteed; don't let your opportunities to glorify God pass by.

Although the story of the Siberian wrestler is heartbreaking in many ways, let's not lose sight of the primary lesson. Don't wait to honor God, because the "perfect opportunity" may never come. Instead, be faithful with whatever opportunities God places before you today.

APPLICATION:

Speaking to others about God can often be a scary thought. A simple way to help overcome these fears is by being prepared. One of the best ways to prepare yourself for opportunities when they arise is by being aware of what God has been doing in your life recently. Take some time to think through how you have seen God work in your life over the past month. Consider the people, places, and situations that have worked together to bring you closer to God. As you think through God's personal and ongoing work in your life, consider how different bits and pieces might provide an opportunity to speak to others about God.

TIP:

Here's an example of what it might sound like to share God's work in your life after a competition: [Fan]: "Great game! What got into you tonight?" [You]: "Thanks. Honestly, this past week God has been reminding me of His love and that really helped me have the right attitude while competing tonight." (Of course, you will want to share insights that are truthful and should never fabricate facts to appear godly.)

BATTLING PRIDE

A gust of dusty wind blew the two high school girls' ponytails into the air. Softball practice had just ended for Hanna and Viviana, and they were taking the opportunity to catch up on all the latest school news. As they sat together on the wooden benches in the dugout, the topic of Viviana's latest hairstyle came up, and Hanna was quick to offer her opinion.

"I love how your hair has looked this week. It must take you forever to get ready in the morning!"

"Well, thanks," Viviana replied bashfully. "Honestly, I haven't thought it looked that great. You would see what a mess it was in the mornings if you were getting up early enough to go to the batting cages like I have. I guess I've just been saving enough time to throw my hair together in the car."

Let's stop there. This is a prime example of what could be called a "humble brag." Viviana used the compliment she received as an opportunity to promote all the practice she was putting in before school. In other words, a "humble brag" is when someone attempts to cover up true pride with a show of humility. If you don't think that sounds biblical, you would be correct, and we don't have to look very hard into the Scriptures to find out why. Proverbs 27:2 says, "Let another praise you, and not your own mouth; a stranger, and not your own lips."

The nice thing about this verse is how simple it is. God doesn't recommend that you check the back of your Bible for a pride ranking scale. There are no *ifs*, *ands*, or *buts* about it. It says, don't praise yourself. First Peter 5:5 further commands believers on this topic: "Clothe yourselves, all of you, with humility toward one another, for 'God opposes the proud but gives grace to the humble.'" Although as Christians we might be more careful to avoid outright boasting, seemingly hidden forms of self-promotion can often sneak their way into our lives.

Looking back at the story of Hanna and Viviana shows one example of a sneaky type of pride. Even though Viviana wasn't walking around arrogantly boasting about her early-morning workouts, she certainly jumped at the opportunity for a bit of self-promotion when it presented itself. Here's the problem—it doesn't matter how you say a prideful comment; pride is pride, regardless of how you package it. It's like trying to put wrapping paper around dog poop. The dog poop is still disgusting; all the wrapping paper does is try to make it look pretty and cover it up. The Scriptures are clear—pride is a sin, and there aren't any exceptions.

APPLICATION:

Battling pride can sometimes prove to be a challenge for Christians. Rather than trying in your own strength to overcome pride, instead make a practice of thankfulness. Next time you find yourself tempted to pride, flip the situation around by considering the many reasons you can be thankful. What you may come to find is that it's practically impossible to be proud and thankful at the same time.

TIP:

As you make a practice of thankfulness, try not to use generic reasons like "God, thank you for my sport." Instead, think more deeply about why you can and should be thankful in your immediate circumstances like "God, thank you for my teammate or coach who cares about me."

WON AN UPSET

Do you know where your success comes from? Is it from your hard work, God's grace, or both? This can be a difficult question for many Christian athletes to answer. So to help better understand this topic, let's consider the words of United States gymnast Lilly Lippeatt, who at the young age of sixteen had already earned her spot on two U. S. national teams.[72] In an interview this is what Lilly had to say about the results of her career: "I myself do not create the results that come from any of my training; [God] does. So everything that I have I have to give to Him."[73] Those are certainly eye-opening words coming from the mouth of an athlete who devotes countless hours of training to her craft. But even if that's Lilly's perspective, is that what the Bible teaches?

Psalm 75:6–7 offers insight into that question: "For not from the east or from the west and not from the wilderness comes lifting up, but it is God who executes judgment, putting down one and lifting up another." These verses make one point undeniably clear. God determines every level of success someone might have. The theme of this passage is continued in 1 Corinthians 15:10, where Paul states, "But by the grace of God I am what I am, and his grace toward me was not in vain. On the contrary, I worked harder than any of them, though it was not I, but the grace of God that is with me." Once again, this verse serves as a necessary reminder that it is by God's grace you achieve what you do—with that said, it is helpful to provide a word of caution here.

Understanding that God is behind your success as a Christian athlete doesn't give you the excuse to be lazy. Certainly your hard work does matter. Did you notice that Paul said, "I worked harder than any of them"? Scripture calls Christ's followers to steward their gifts well. This is why it may be helpful to think of your hard work as God's working through you, which leads us to where we started.

If we think back to Lippeatt, it's clear that reaching her level of skill required a high level of hard work. However, as she acknowledged, if God had not been behind her successes and working through her efforts, they wouldn't have happened.

Although this topic can sometimes be challenging to understand, the lesson from these verses is less about how your work and God's work unite and more about understanding your role in the equation: work hard, enjoy what God brings, and give Him the praise!

APPLICATION:

After reading this devotion, you may be tempted to think there's no reason to celebrate a success when you weren't the one ultimately behind it. This is certainly not the case. Rather than letting the thought of God's role in your success as an athlete discourage you, consider what a great privilege it is that God has granted you the success He has. The only way to truly enjoy success as God intends is by understanding it for what it is—a gift from God. And if it's a gift, then it's only fitting to give God the praise.

TIP:

Keep in mind that praising God is an action, not a feeling. It will be helpful to remember this because you might not feel like praising God in all situations.

THE MORNING AFTER COMPETING

Bruises, scrapes, and sore muscles are friendly reminders that you competed the day before. Although these aches might not feel the best now, have you ever noticed that you rarely think about these pains during competition? It's quite impressive how the amount of abuse your body can take goes completely unnoticed in the heat of action. Of course, you may feel the occasional bump or bruise, but when you start to compete they are put out of mind. Instead, you're focused on something much more important: winning.

Odds are, none of this information is new to you. But now that we've covered an experience felt by many athletes, the stage is set to look at two passages of Scripture relevant to this subject. Let's start with Romans 8:18, where Paul says, "For I consider that the sufferings of this present time are not worth comparing with the glory that is to be revealed to us." Paul's encouragement is clear; the pains and troubles of this life are insignificant in view of eternity. Paul further establishes this truth in our second passage of Scripture, 2 Corinthians 4:16–18: "So we do not lose heart. Though our outer self is wasting away, our inner self is being renewed day by day. For this light momentary affliction is preparing for us an eternal weight of glory beyond all comparison, as we look not to the things that are seen but to the things that are unseen. For the things that are seen are transient, but the things that are unseen are eternal." With these verses fresh in our minds, we can now consider how they connect with our topic from the beginning.

Much how the bruises, scrapes, and sore muscles faced in competition lose their significance when your mind is on winning, the stresses, pains, and troubles of your life can also lose their significance when your mind is on eternal things. It's not that the difficulties disappear but that you're focused on something much more important.

Next time you find yourself facing pains, troubles, difficulties, or sufferings, remember: this life is not all there is. If you're a believer, you have something far greater than an athletic victory to look forward to; you have eternal life.

APPLICATION:

As you learned above, focusing on eternal things can be a powerful tool to direct your mind away from the sufferings of this life. Another helpful practice is remembering that you're not alone. All across the world, fellow brothers and sisters in Christ are going through extreme forms of suffering because of their faith in Christ. Hebrews 13:3 says it's your responsibility as a Christian to remember them. Open a world map and pick a country that you will commit to begin praying for on a regular basis. You may find it helpful to print off a picture of this country and place it in your Bible as a reminder.

TIP:

Operation World is a helpful resource that can share with you specific ways to pray for your chosen country. You can quickly get started by searching for your country on the Operation World website (https://operationworld.org/).

A RECORD WAS BROKEN

The sport of running changed forever on May 6, 1954. It was on that day that Roger Bannister, a twenty-five-year-old Oxford medical student, crossed the finish line of a one-mile race, clocking a time of 3:59.04. Bannister became the first person to run a mile in under four minutes and in turn broke a barrier that doctors and scientists had previously thought was humanly impossible.

As incredible as the feat was, it was only one month later when the barrier would be broken again, this time by an Australian with an even better time of 3:57.90. As if that weren't enough, only three years after Bannister's mile run fifteen others had added their names to the list of runners to dip under the four-minute mark.[74] Fast-forward ten years and Jim Ryun became the first high schooler to accomplish the task.[75] By the time the fiftieth anniversary of Bannister's mile rolled around, in America alone over 250 runners had crossed the one-mile finish line in under four minutes.[76]

Proof is powerful, and the story of Bannister clearly points to that fact. Once he proved that cracking a four-minute mile was achievable, the barrier was broken again and again. This, of course, was no coincidence. Bannister had become living evidence to runners across the world that accomplishing the task was possible.

Although this story might not inspire you to try running a sub-four-minute mile yourself, it does provide excellent starting blocks to reflect on Hebrews 12:1, which says, "Therefore, since we are surrounded by so great a cloud of witnesses, let us also lay aside every weight, and sin which clings so closely, and let us run with endurance the race that is set before us." When Hebrews 12:1 speaks of a "cloud of witnesses," it refers to the godly men and women in the Scriptures who lived lives of faith in God. Think Noah, David, Rahab, and the like. At first glance it may appear that this verse is saying these men and women of Scripture are in heaven cheering you on. In actuality, what this verse teaches is much more inspiring. Hebrews 12:1 is a call for readers to run their race of faith with the encouragement that, by faith in Christ, countless other faithful Christians have completed the race. That call is where Bannister's story ties in.

Once Bannister proved that circling the track four times in under four minutes was achievable, runners no longer saw the four-minute barrier as an impossible feat. Similarly, the saints from the Scriptures have run the race of faith themselves, leaving you evidence that the race is possible. Their story may look different than yours, but they provide the encouragement that by faith in Christ you can complete your race.

APPLICATION:

Take a moment to pick one of your favorite Bible characters from the Old or New Testament to go back through and review their story. If that person's story spans a large portion of Scripture, try finding a timeline of the major events that took place throughout his or her life. As you review your chosen character's life, look for ways that person ran his or her race through faith in God. You might try answering questions like "In what ways did [character] live by faith?" or "What types of adversities did [character] face? How did he or she respond?" If you're a note-taker, you might jot down a few observations you can reference later.

TIP:

Even the failures of our favorite Bible characters can teach us important lessons about the race of faith.

ASSESSING YOUR ACTIONS

According to the *Meriam Webster's Dictionary*, the definition of *competition* is "the act or process of competing"[77]; the definition of *opponent* is "one that takes an opposite position"[78]; and the definition of *scoreboard* is "a large board for displaying the score of a game or match."[79] Now it's your turn...

If you were to open a dictionary and turn to a page with your name on it, what would your definition be? It's fine to take a moment to think about this. If you're being honest, what words would go next to your name? Is it something you would be ashamed of, embarrassed about, or maybe pleased with? You and God might be the only two who know your definition, but the Bible can tell you what your definition should be.

There are many places we could look to see how God defines Christians in the Bible, and Galatians 5:22–23 is one of them. In this passage Paul describes the various attributes that should characterize a Christian: "But the fruit of the Spirit is love, joy, peace, patience, kindness, goodness, faithfulness, gentleness, self-control."

These verses give an unquestionably high standard to live by, and that's why the beginning of this passage is so important. If you are a Christian, you have the Spirit of God living inside you. That doesn't just make these characteristics possible for you but it also makes them a part of who you are. We see this clearly laid out only two short verses later in Galatians 5:25: "If we live by the Spirit, let us also keep in step with the Spirit." The fruits of the Spirit are inside you; now it's your job to cultivate them. For that reason, your definition is different than those from the start.

Unlike the definitions from the beginning, which are complete and final, your definition isn't. The definition of who you are is still being written, and it depends on how you live today. Will you culti-vate the fruits of the Spirit God has put inside you, or are you content with less?

APPLICATION:

Take a moment to write a personal definition. As you do, try your best to write what is true about yourself and not only what you want to hear. Once you've finished, look back at the list found in Galatians 5:22–23 to see where you match up and where you don't. (Although you might not use the exact words as the vers-es, would you say those qualities are visible in your life?)

TIP:

Do you want to take things a step further? Ask a close friend or family member to write an open and honest definition of you.

CONQUERING ENVY

*C*rash! Broken glass was everywhere, and a brand-new opening had been created between the art room and the school playground. A large group of high schoolers stood silently, staring at the wreckage. Before the group could make their escape, the art teacher stepped outside with a baseball in her hand and a frown on her face.

"Uh-oh," said one in the group.

"I told you guys that playing ultimate frisbee with a baseball was a bad idea," another one whispered.

You can fill in the rest of the story with your imagination. The point of this story isn't about punishment; it's about purpose. There's a reason you shouldn't play ultimate frisbee with a baseball. It doesn't work. Specific things are designed for specific jobs. A baseball is designed to be pitched, hit, and caught with a glove, not thrown around like a frisbee. When you take something that is intended for one purpose and use it for another, you might experience a lot of frustration and damage but you won't get from it what you were meant to.

This leads us to an extraordinary truth found in Ephesians 2:10: "For we are his workmanship, created in Christ Jesus for good works, which God prepared beforehand, that we should walk in them." Let's quickly break this verse down. It's saying that you are a special work of God, intentionally shaped by God for specific good works that God has prepared for you to live out. The implications of this verse are huge.

As a child of God, you are unique and incredible in more ways than you can imagine. But when you envy others, wishing you were in their shoes, you're being distracted from God's design for your life. Trying to live out someone else's mission instead of your own is like trying to play ultimate frisbee with a baseball; it doesn't work because you weren't made for it.

Fortunately, that's not how it has to be. It's up to you to decide. Do you want to experience the incredible blessing and joy of living as God intends? Then choose to live with a mindset of daily faithfulness, striving to be faithful with the purposes and plans that God places before you today.

APPLICATION:

The next time a thought of envy plagues your mind, flip it on its head and use it as a reminder to begin looking for the good works God has prepared for you today. As you do, you might find it helpful to consider the following three questions: "Where has God placed me right now?" "What roles/responsibilities has God given me right now?" and in light of those things, "How can I best serve God right now?"

TIP:

Do you want to take an even further step toward conquering envy? Start praying for the person you're envious of.

FRUSTRATED WITH THE SEASON

Jeremy had had enough. It was his first week back on the court since he tore his ACL nine months ago, and things were not going well. For starters, his basketball team had lost all four games they had played that week in a tournament. On top of that, Jeremy, who used to be the star player, was barely getting any playing time because his coach wanted to be careful. If that weren't enough, it was Jeremy's senior year, and unless a miracle happened, his team would not be qualifying for state competition.

Needless to say, Jeremy was not in a great mood when he got into his parents' car after his team's final loss on Friday night. Directing all his attention to his phone, Jeremy tuned out his surroundings until his mom broke the silence.

"Well, Jeremy, you know, there's always the next game."

Without taking his eyes off the screen, Jeremy didn't respond.

His mom continued. "And I overheard the coach's wife saying that he's planning on playing you even more next week."

Jeremy paused, let out a sigh, and then stated flatly, "Whatever, Mom."

Frustrated. Angry. Bored. All three? Sometimes as athletes, we know that things don't go the way we want. Maybe the season is seeming to drag on, or you aren't competing at the high level you expected. Or maybe like Jeremy your motivation has dropped to a level of being "whatever." Although it would be easier to mope around and sulk in self-pity during times like this, the Bible calls believers to a higher standard. As a matter of fact, the Scriptures cover "whatever" situations quite extensively. Cue the three "whatevers" of the Bible.

The first comes from Colossians 3:17, which says, "And whatever you do, in word or deed, do everything in the name of the Lord Jesus, giving thanks to God the Father through him." Number two comes only a few verses later in Colossians 3:23–24, when Paul says, "Whatever you do, work heartily, as for the Lord and not for men, knowing that from the Lord you will receive the inheritance as your reward. You are serving the Lord Christ." Finally, the last passage is found in 1 Corinthians 10:31: "So, whether you eat or drink, or whatever you do, do all to the glory of God."

Right now you might have the same attitude Jeremy did, but that can change. These three verses give clear instructions for how you are to act in "whatever" situation you find yourself in, including your sport. You're to do all things "in the name of the Lord"; "giving thanks"; working "heartily, as for the Lord"; and doing "all to the glory of God." Understandably, this is much easier said than done. Thankfully, God hasn't merely given you these commands; He's given you the grace to obey through the power of the Holy Spirit inside you.

APPLICATION:

As a Christian, it's crucial that you have a faith that's bigger than your feelings. While feelings are a gift from God, notice that none of the verses deal with feelings; they deal with actions. Although you might continue to feel frustrated or discouraged moving forward, make the decision now that you are going to choose to obey the commands of the three "whatever" verses as your season continues. You may not be able to control your circumstances, but by God's grace, you can control how you respond.

TIP:

Changing how you act can often lead to a change in how you feel.

AFTER A
HARD LOSS

Most athletes take losing very seriously, and there may be no one who exemplified this mindset better than tennis legend Serena Williams. Widely considered the greatest female tennis player of all time, Williams created a tennis legacy that was marked by significantly more wins than losses. However, when Williams did take an *L*, she didn't take it lightly. Williams described her perspective on losing when questioned during a press conference in 2015.

"I don't want to talk about how disappointing it is for me," she said. "If you have any other questions, I'm open for that."[80] This verbal exchange with reporters was later featured as part of a Gatorade exclusive podcast interview with Williams fittingly titled "Serena Williams: I'm Not Supposed to Lose."[81]

Throughout her career Williams put to words the attitude many competitors have toward defeat. Yet as significant as losing a sports competition may be, losing the battle over your mind is even more so. This mental battle is a contest that is determined by what you let influence your thinking: the world or the Word.

Scripture is clear on the opposite effects these two sources have when it charges believers in Romans 12:2, "Do not be conformed to this world, but be transformed by the renewal of your mind, that by testing you may discern what is the will of God, what is good and acceptable and perfect." The point is simple. While you live in this world, one of two things will transform your mindset. It will either be the w-o-r-l-d or God's W-o-r-d. The only difference between the two is the single letter *L*, but it makes a profound difference.

In the same way that Williams had a deep-seated hatred toward a loss blemishing her tennis career, the Christian should have a disgust toward the worLd tarnishing his or her thinking.

As you go about your daily life, your mindset is constantly being shaped. What do you typically think about throughout the day? What are you spending your time on? Who do you tend to act like? Ultimately your answers to these questions may reveal whether the w-o-r-l-d or the W-o-r-d is transforming you.

APPLICATION:

Total the number of hours you spend training and competing in your sport each week. Once you've got your number, repeat the same process, this time calculating the amount of time you spend reading God's Word, praying, and going to church. Compare these two numbers, noting the differences. If the time spent renewing your mind is sorely lacking, there are many creative ways you can improve. For example, try praying instead of listening to music on the way to school. Another great option is listening to sermons or Christian podcasts as you do chores or yard work.

TIP:

You don't need to feel convicted that you should spend the exact same amount of time spiritually training your mind that you spend training for your sport. If your desire is for mental renewal, the time you spend doing those activities will naturally increase.

RESPONDING TO ADVERSITY

Heading into the eighteenth hole of the UIL Texas State Golfing Tournament, senior golfer Philip Hues prepared to tee off with a one-stroke lead against the field. All that separated the three-time defending champion from a fourth title was the final 442-yard-par four.

After carefully aligning his swing, Philip connected his driver with the golf ball. Immediately his face turned sour, and it quickly became evident why. Veering far right of the fairway, Philip's ball landed on a sidewalk and bounced into the rough, leaving the ball in an odd location. Unfortunately for Philip, what followed was a series of mistakes, first hitting a tree and then landing in a bunker—ultimately resulting in Philip relinquishing the state title to a lower-classman.

Philip's string of errors in the state tournament is a prime example of the power that one mistake can have. His mistake was not a bad shot but letting that bad shot lead to another and another. As surprising as it may sound, how you respond to adversity may have a greater impact on your life than the adversity itself.

This is where having God as your Father comes with an upper hand. God's Word provides you as a Christian with two extraordinary promises that enable you to respond to adversity well. Beginning in Psalm 55:22 we read, "Cast your burden on the Lord, and he will sustain you; he will never permit the righteous to be moved." A related passage comes in Isaiah 26:3: "You keep him in perfect peace whose mind is stayed on you, because he trusts in you." These verses invite Christians to turn to God when facing difficulty and trustingly cast whatever they're facing on Him. For those who obey, God promises to provide stability and peace—two beautiful qualities that we should keep in mind as we return to our story from the beginning.

When Hues teed off on the final hole of the state tournament, what initially appeared as simply a poor shot spiraled into a domino of blunders that ultimately led to defeat. The problem was not Philip's initial shot but how he responded to the shot. Likewise, when you face adversity, the outcome of your struggle can go one of two ways. You can let the adversity drag you further down into more uncertainty and anxiety, or you can give it to the Lord and trust in Him to provide the stability and peace you're looking for.

APPLICATION:

Grab an unused cardboard box and write "God Box" on the front. Whenever you feel burdened about a situation you're facing, grab a piece of paper and write down the problem. With your paper in hand, prayerfully bring the burden before the Lord, asking for His peace, and then place the paper inside the box. If you find that you're continuing to concern yourself about the situation, go back and take the paper out of the box until you're ready to cast it back on the Lord. This will serve as a visual representation of what's going on in your heart and mind.

TIP:

As with many good practices, the "God Box" will only be a distraction if you let it become a religious ritual rather than a helpful reminder for your heart and mind.

SILENCING COMPARISON

It's Friday afternoon, and the cheerleaders are holding a pep rally to kick off the fall sports season. The gym is packed with students, and much to your surprise, you're selected to represent your class in a head-to-head competition. As you make your way to the center of the court, the cheerleaders in charge gather you and the other class representatives into a huddle to explain the game. It's a race to see who can jump the farthest inside a potato sack in ten seconds. But there's a twist. Everyone will be starting at a different location.

Of the four racers, one will start at the baseline, one at the free-throw line, one at the three-point line, and the last at the half-court line. Your starting point depends on the card you draw. Luckily, you're first up, and after digging your hand into the basket, you confidently pull out what you expect to be your ticket to the half-court line. As you unfold the piece of paper, both shock and disappointment spread across your face. The word "BASELINE" is written in bright purple letters on the small sliver of paper.

You shuffle to the baseline and place your feet in the empty potato sack. As you prepare for the start of the race, frustrated thoughts are rattling through your mind. *This isn't fair. This isn't even a race.* Before you can continue, the lead cheerleader cheerfully raises her arms and blows an air horn, signaling the start of the race.

There's no question that this race sounds unfair. But as unfair as it sounds, it serves to illustrate a reality that is clearly taught in Paul's letters to the Corinthians.

Let's begin with 1 Corinthians 4:7, where Paul says, "For who sees anything different in you? What do you have that you did not receive? If then you received it, why do you boast as if you did not receive it?" The point Paul is getting at is clear: everything you have, you have been given. In His wisdom God has graciously distributed different circumstances, opportunities, and talents to each human being.

Moving from that point, we come to 2 Corinthians 10:12, where Paul expresses, "Not that we dare to classify or compare ourselves with some of those who are commending themselves. But when they measure themselves by one another and compare themselves with one another, they are without understanding." Underlying Paul's words in this passage is the simple fact that comparison is foolish. Recognizing this leads us back to why comparison doesn't work.

At its core, comparison is rooted in measuring one person against another. The problem is that not everyone is on the same playing field. As we've seen from the above verses, the Christian life is like the pep-rally race. God has gifted every individual in different ways, so in a sense, everyone is starting at a different place. Nothing good comes from sinful comparison. That's why as a Christian, you are called to avoid it. When you compare, you lose.

APPLICATION:

Next time you're tempted to compare, use it as an opportunity to put into practice the command of Galatians 6:4: "But let each one test his own work, and then his reason to boast will be in himself alone and not in his neighbor." This verse is a call to take your eyes off others and put them on yourself. Rather than comparing your life with your peers, consider yourself before God. How well are you living your own Christian life?

TIP:

It's helpful to remember that God's kingdom runs on a different value system than the world's does. For the Christian it's not about "how far you make it" in this life but rather how faithful you were to the King.

CONFESSING SIN

Thick tension filled the room. Olivia, the starting libero, sat cross-armed, silently staring at the ground with three days of irritation hardened on her face. Sitting directly opposite the high schooler behind a large wooden desk was the head volleyball coach, who appeared equally annoyed.

"Okay, I'm sorry." Olivia broke the silence. "What I did was wrong. We both know that. I let my anger get the best of me and shouldn't have."

As Olivia paused, her coach noticed tears beginning to well up in Olivia's eyes.

"Will you please forgive me?" She had a noticeable change in emotion.

After two calm breaths, Olivia's coach responded gently, "Of course I will, Olivia."

Without another word, the athlete and coach exchanged hugs, having a newly restored relationship.

The next day one of Olivia's teammates approached her. "Did you make up with Coach yesterday?"

"Yeah, did the tear stains on my face give it away?" Olivia asked.

"No. You and Coach just seemed to be off all week. Well, until yesterday."

Confession is not a popular topic, and there's no question why. Typically confession is an unpleasant experience for everyone involved. Yet as difficult as confession can be, it's also biblical. For this reason it's important that as Christians we have a proper understanding of this rather unpopular topic. Let's briefly compare two verses that will hopefully give us a little better insight into confession.

The first comes from Colossians 2:13: "And you, who were dead in your trespasses and the uncircumcision of your flesh, God made alive together with him, having forgiven us all our trespasses." For a Christian, this is a simple and comforting verse. It relays the message that God has forgiven all of your past, present, and future sins because of Christ's death on the cross. They're gone.

That would be a great place to stop, but 1 John 1:9 adds more to the conversation: "If we confess our sins, he is faithful and just to forgive us our sins and to cleanse us from all unrighteousness." Wait—didn't Colossians 2:13 say God has already forgiven our sins? If that's the case, why do you need to confess them? The answer relates to why Olivia needed to apologize to her volleyball coach.

When you confess your sin to God, that means you are saying the same thing about your sin that God does. You're agreeing with Him that your sin was wrong and needs to be dealt with. Until you confess your sins to God, your relationship with Him is strained—much like Olivia's relationship was strained with her coach. Of course, having a strained relationship with God makes you no less His child than Olivia's strained relationship with her coach stopped making her one of the volleyball players. However, it does mean you're missing out on the close relationship that God desires to have with you.

APPLICATION:

You can't turn back the clock and undo a sin you've already committed, but you can take steps to restore your relationship with God. If you have a particular sin pressing upon your heart, confess it to God right now.

TIP:

If others have been affected by your sin, it would be a good idea to apologize for the wrong you've done to them and ask for their forgiveness.

CAME DOWN TO THE WIRE

They call it the Music City Miracle. Trailing the Buffalo Bills by one in the AFC Wild Card round, the Tennessee Titans were set to receive a kickoff with sixteen seconds left in the game.[82] Rather than doing what most would expect in a situation like this, kneeling the ball and attempting a Hail Mary pass, the Titans pulled out a special play that they had stored away for a moment exactly like this.

After receiving the pooch kick from Buffalo, Titan Lorenzo Neal quickly handed the ball into the hands of tight end Frank Wycheck, a rather unusual maneuver for a kickoff. With the ball in hand, Wycheck began his trek down the field, eyeing the approaching defense as they drew near. Before any of the Bills were close enough to tackle him, Wycheck stepped back and threw a cross-field pass right into the arms of Kevin Dyson—a Titan player who had been hiding out. Dyson latched onto the ball and raced into the end zone, winning the game.[83] This play has gone down as one of the greatest trick plays in history[84] and for a good reason. It's a play you won't see every day, and it leads us to a passage of Scripture you won't see every day either.

In 1 Chronicles 16:11 we find these words "Seek the Lord and his strength; seek his presence continually!" As simple as this command is, the implications are far-reaching. As Christians we can sometimes treat God like the Tennessee Titans treated their trick play, only to be pulled out for special moments. Unfortunately, those moments can sometimes be few and far between.

To be quite blunt, God does not want children who forget about Him in everyday life only to call on Him when they need a miracle. There's no such thing as a part-time Christian. You're either a Christian all the time or not a Christian at all. Consider where you stand on this subject. If someone were to look at your life, would they see that you seek God "continually"?

APPLICATION:

The principle behind this lesson is relatively straightforward, and so is the application. Take a moment to reflect on when you tend to most often forget about God in your everyday life. Does it tend to happen at a certain time of day? If so, set a reminder on your phone to notify you with a verse or a phrase (such as, "seek God" or "1 Chronicles 16:11") that can draw your attention back to God. If you've come to realize that you tend to regularly forget about God numerous times throughout the day, consider setting multiple reminders with different phrases and/or verses.

TIP:

Some reminder apps offer the ability to set a reminder on repeat for the same time every day. Utilizing a tool like this will be much more convenient than recreating the same daily reminder(s).

ENCOUNTERING CRISIS

The roar of the crowd was deafening. It was Friday night, and the Brookeville Bears men's basketball team had managed to come back from the wrong side of a first-half blowout to find themselves within one point of victory. Having the ball in their possession and ten seconds left in regulation, the Bears' head coach called a time-out to prepare his players for one final play. With passion and precision, the coach meticulously colored his clipboard with bright arrows as the players huddled, shaking their heads in agreement. When the huddle broke and the game resumed, the Bears' head coach watched in horror as the final play unfolded.

Tweet! Dominic, the star point guard, took the inbounding pass and quickly deviated from the plan, driving hard to the basket and looking to create an opening down low with his ball-handling skills. Realizing that his makeshift play had gotten him nowhere and that time was running out, Dominic threw up a last-ditch shot that fell well short of the rim, leaving the Bears with an "almost" comeback.

From this story it's easy to see what Dominic did was wrong. However, more important to our conversation is why Dominic's actions were wrong. Dominic may have been the star player, but he wasn't the coach. As a player, Dominic's role was to be coached, not to be the coach. Unfortunately, this sort of thing doesn't only happen in sports.

Christians can sometimes pick up on the same attitude that Dominic displayed in their attitude toward God. In Jeremiah 17:5–8 we are warned of the negative consequences that can come from doing this.

> *Thus says the LORD: "Cursed is the man who trusts in man and makes flesh his strength, whose heart turns away from the LORD. He is like a shrub in the desert, and shall not see any good come. He shall dwell in the parched places of the wilderness, in*

an uninhabited salt land. Blessed is the man who trusts in the Lord, *whose trust is the* Lord. *He is like a tree planted by water, that sends out its roots by the stream, and does not fear when heat comes, for its leaves remain green, and is not anxious in the year of drought, for it does not cease to bear fruit."*

These verses clearly depict two drastically different outcomes that result from either trusting in God or failing to do so. This brings us back to the start.

When Dominic stepped out of his rightful role as a player and instead fulfilled the role of coach, his actions showed that his trust wasn't in his coach but in himself. In a similar way, it would be good for us to consider our own attitude toward God. When we lack trust in God or take any situation into our own hands, we are doing much worse than Dominic. We are trying to take the role of God.

APPLICATION:

When you encounter a crisis, take a moment to sit down and draw up two plays on a piece of paper. To begin, summarize your problem at the top of the page and then write how you would naturally respond to the situation. This will represent the first play. Flip the page over and repeat the process; this time, consider what the Bible says about your situation and write the solution you believe God would have. This will represent the second play. Once you're done, compare the two plays and consider the outcome each would bring.

TIP:

If you're struggling to determine what God's play might look like for your crisis, try looking up various Bible verses that speak to your situation.

MADE A BIG MISTAKE

"What just happened?!" The junior varsity hockey coach could barely believe his eyes. It was Tuesday night, and the Ark City Bulldogs were facing off against the Brecksville Knights. With Ark City leading 1–0 and the first period drawing to a close, a blocked pass by the Knights created an opening for a quick play down the ice. Breaking into the open, number 20 from the Knights quickly glided the puck down the rink and sent a centering pass directly at Jake Hulse, a defender for Ark City. As the puck flew by, Hulse snatched the black disk out of the air and attempted to clear it to the other side of the rink. Instead, Hulse's throw went directly past his own goalie straight into the Bulldogs' net. The blunder was so unbelievable that many of the fans struggled to understand what happened. Hulse had literally thrown the puck into his own goal, and his bright-red face made it clear that he knew he had made a big mistake.

Hulse's blooper is not something you see every day, and for good reason. To score for the other team is absolutely absurd. You might even say, as absurd as it is for a Christian to sin. First Peter 4:1–5 explains this logic.

> *Since therefore Christ suffered in the flesh, arm your-selves with the same way of thinking, for whoever has suffered in the flesh has ceased from sin, so as to live for the rest of the time in the flesh no longer for human passions but for the will of God. For the time that is past suffices for doing what the Gentiles want to do, living in sensuality, passions, drunken-ness, orgies, drinking parties, and lawless idolatry. With respect to this they are surprised when you do not join them in the same flood of debauchery,*

*and they malign you; but they will give account to
him who is ready to judge the living and the dead.*

The message of these verses is clear Christians shouldn't sin. Unfortunately, in some situations, putting that message into practice can feel like a shot to the gut. That's why looking at it from a slightly different angle can help.

When Hulse scored a goal for the opponent, it was a complete fluke. The coach was baffled, the fans were dismayed, and Hulse was visibly embarrassed. If that's the case with a mistake like that, why then would a Christian make the mistake of sinning? When you join in with the sins of the world, in essence, you're scoring goals for the enemy. Although the concept of avoiding sin is likely something you've heard before, the challenge here is to change how you think about it.

APPLICATION:

Set aside a few minutes before bed each night to reflect on how you thought, spoke, and acted throughout the day. During these moments ponder the following questions:

- Were my thoughts pleasing God?
- Did my words bring God delight?
- Have my actions been pure in God's sight?

Creating a habit of self-reflection can prove helpful in assessing your life at a heart level.

TIP:

Moments of reflection can become very discouraging if they cause you to take your eyes off Christ. Be sure to end every session by remembering that Christ has paid for your sins and has made it possible for you to change.

RESPONDING TO PRAISE

Heading into the 2020 United States Olympic Team Trials for track and field, anticipation was building around 400-meter hurdle superstar Sydney McLaughlin. Five years earlier, McLaughlin had stunned the world by qualifying for her first Olympic games at the young age of sixteen. Now twenty-one, McLaughlin was back and ready to qualify for her second Olympics.

When the renowned hurdler took to the track for her premier event, the 400-meter hurdles, the country watched in awe as McLaughlin did what had never been done before. ESPN covered the scene: "Sydney McLaughlin broke the world record in the women's 400-meter hurdles on Sunday night and qualified for her second Olympic Games . . . becoming the first woman to break the 52-second barrier."[85]

The day following her record-breaking performance, McLaughlin took to Instagram to share her thoughts:

> *Weeks like these are some of the hardest in a track athletes [sic] life. The mental strain of preparing for the rounds in order to solidify your spot is heavy enough. But the amount of weight the Lord took off my shoulders, is the reason I could run so freely yesterday. . . . I no longer run for self recognition, but to reflect His perfect will that is already set in stone. . . . Records come and go. The glory of God is eternal. Thank you Father [sic].*[86]

McLaughlin's words are powerful, and they reveal a key principle about the word *glory* clearly taught in the Scriptures, a principle that holds real significance for any athlete seeking to respond to praise in the right way.

In the Old Testament the word for *glory* could literally mean "weight."[87] This suggests that all glory has weight to it—a type of weight that no human being was designed to bear. Psalm 115:1 offers a strong demonstration of this truth when it says, "Not to us, O LORD, not to us, but to your name give glory, for the sake of your steadfast love and your faithfulness!"

As an athlete, you were not designed to absorb praise but to reflect it. Although you may not be able to change the fact that others will praise you, you can certainly choose how you will respond. That is why Psalm 115:1 commands believers to "give glory" to God. How you respond to praise may not seem significant at the moment, but in the end it will impact you on a soul level. McLaughlin is a prime example of what it looks like to respond the right way, and because of her response, she was able to experience the lifted burden that comes from giving God the glory.

APPLICATION:

Compare and contrast how King Herod received praise in Acts 12:20-23 with how Paul received praise in Acts 14:1-18. The stories provide a real-life example of two drastically different responses when faced with public glory.

TIP:

It's important to remember that giving God glory includes all your actions as an athlete, not only the words you say after a competition.

DISHEARTENED BY DEFEAT

Sniff, sniff. A pool of tears was beginning to form on the cold concrete floor. Sitting alone in the dark locker room was a high school senior with his face buried deeply in his hands. "And now for your men's cross-country championships." A faint echo from outside the door could be heard. The senior didn't move. A pair of mud-stained cross-country spikes sat next to him on the bench, covering the form of a second-place medal.

Clunk. The locker room door was thrown open, and a voice shouted, "Hey, hurry up! They're doing the awards ceremony!"

The senior looked up from the dark floor to an opening of light pouring through the doorway. "I didn't come here for second. I came for first." Silence followed as the senior's words sunk in.

There's a lot we could learn from this story. So rather than focus our attention on what the senior did, we're going to look more specifically at why he did it. To put it bluntly, in sports there's only one first place, and the senior didn't win that spot. Although that may seem like a rather unusual thought going into a passage of Scripture, in the end it will connect.

In Matthew 22:37–38 Jesus said, "You shall love the Lord your God with all your heart and with all your soul and with all your mind. This is the great and first commandment." In this passage Jesus gave His followers a simple command: to love God first. When Jesus said this, He understood the exclusiveness of His command. Jesus lived in the same world we do—a world full of things competing for our hearts. For that reason, Jesus was making clear that God is not interested in taking a secondary role in your life. He requires first place. This is where Jesus's words tie in with the story from earlier.

Although God is far different from a high school senior who's upset about taking second, the story can at least give us a taste of the grief and righteous anger God feels when you give Him second place in your life—grief because sin is always grievous to God, and He desires for you to find your greatest joy in Him; righteous anger because you are robbing Him of what is rightfully His.

It's easy to think you love God first when all your needs are met, you get your way, and things are going well, but when any of those factors are disrupted, it can often reveal God's true position in your heart.

APPLICATION:

In the moments you face defeat this season, use the opportunity to assess the position of your heart. Does your response show true love for God first, or have comforts been hiding a different reality? It's important to acknowledge when your heart is out of line so you can take steps to change it.

TIP:

There's nothing wrong with winning first—as long as winning does not take first place in your heart.

THINGS AREN'T GOING YOUR WAY

Her name was Perfect, and she was the type of person everyone dreams of being. Born into a wealthy family, with excellent grades, an attractive appearance, a loveable personality, fashionable and trendy clothes, natural physical abilities, a complete sports skillset, and a luxury car, Perfect had everything you could imagine. Grades, check. Style, check. Sports, check.

Take a moment and put yourself in Perfect's shoes. Envision what it would be like to have everything you have ever wanted—to be Perfect.

So, if you were Perfect, would you still want Jesus? Resist the urge to quickly think *Yes!* and move on; there's more to this. Things like money and trendy clothes are much less alluring when they're seen from a distance. Likewise, being the best athlete in the state might not seem like that big of a deal, until you are. The probing question we're getting at here is this: How precious is Jesus to you?

In the Scriptures we find a wonderful example of someone who resembles the perfect life described above. His name was the apostle Paul. In Philippians 3:4–6 Paul wrote, "If anyone else thinks he has reason for confidence in the flesh, I have more: circumcised on the eighth day, of the people of Israel, of the tribe of Benjamin, a Hebrew of Hebrews; as to the law, a Pharisee; as to zeal, a persecutor of the church; as to righteousness under the law, blameless."

Based on Paul's self-description, you might as well call him Perfect instead of Paul. Yes, Paul had everything going for him. How did he respond? In Philippians 3:7 Paul went on to answer, "But whatever gain I had, I counted as loss for the sake of Christ. Indeed, I count everything as loss because of the surpassing worth of knowing Christ."

Paul decided that Christ was more important than everything he had. To Paul, Christ was most precious. So back to our question from earlier. How precious is Jesus to you? Your answer will make all the difference.

APPLICATION:

Picture what your life would be like without Jesus. If you can think "At least I would still have . . . [fill in the blank]," then it's a good indicator that whatever "that" might be is too precious to you. Moving forward, tuck the following phrase in your back pocket for times when you notice that anything other than Christ is starting to grab at your heart: "Jesus is better than [blank] because. . ." (The deeper the thought you put into answering that phrase, the greater the results will be.)

TIP:

Here's a sample statement, filling in the blank from above: "Jesus is better than popularity because popularity is something I must work to maintain, but Jesus loves me unconditionally."

FOLLOWING A POOR PERFORMANCE

We are about to briefly explore the meaning of a term commonly used in many professional sports leagues: a *salary cap*. In basic terms, a salary cap limits what any one team can pay for all its players.[88] As a basic example, let's say the salary cap set by Major League Soccer is one million dollars. That means every professional soccer team in the league can spend no more than one million dollars on all players' salaries combined. With the intended purpose of keeping overall costs down, the salary cap can serve an important purpose. However, this purpose has often caused many challenges in team dynamics.[89]

When you consider that teams are limited when it comes to paying players, it becomes clear why game day performance is so important. If a professional athlete performs well, his or her value for the team literally goes up. If that athlete performs poorly, it goes down. This can cause various team issues because when one player is paid more, that leaves less money for the rest of the team.

Ironically, salary caps serve as a visual representation of what typically happens in the minds of athletes at every level. According to the world's value system, when one athlete performs better than another, his or her value goes up, and all the competitors' value goes down, not in terms of money but actual self-worth. This is a great tragedy because nowhere does this align with God's Word and yet many Christians unknowingly approve of this thinking.

Thankfully, we have only to look at a simple prayer offered by David in the Old Testament to understand God's much better value system. In 1 Chronicles 29:11–13 David prayed,

> *Yours, O Lord, is the greatness and the power and*
> *the glory and the victory and the majesty, for all*

*that is in the heavens and in the earth is yours.
Yours is the kingdom, O L*ORD, *and you are exalted
as head above all. Both riches and honor come
from you, and you rule over all. In your hand are
power and might, and in your hand it is to make
great and to give strength to all. And now we
thank you, our God, and praise your glorious name.*

These verses express that when it comes to God, He has no "salary cap" and can give freely to all. This stands in stark contrast to the world's mindset. In the world's thinking, there's only so much value out there. It's as if the world has a value cap placed on it. If you're not the person gaining value, you're losing it. But as David shows, the Bible teaches something much different: God has made all people valuable, and that isn't dependent on how you or someone else performs.

APPLICATION:

One way to help put this topic into practice is by complimenting those who performed well and encouraging those who didn't following a competition. Moving forward, make an extra effort to build this practice into your post-competition routine, regardless of how you performed.

TIP:

Personally approaching a competitor or teammate to offer a genuine compliment goes much further than simply saying "good game" as you pass by in the high-five line.

FINISHED WITH
HIGH SCHOOL SPORTS

Every two years the best athletes from around the globe gather together to contest their skill, speed, and endurance in the prestigious Olympic Games. As a tradition, both the Summer and Winter Olympics open the days of competition with the highly celebrated Olympic ceremony. Central to the ceremony's proceedings is the inaugural lighting of the Olympic torch, a moment that holds great significance, owing to the journey each torch takes to get there.

Beginning in ruins of the ancient Olympia, each Olympic torch is lit by the sun's rays and then transported to the country hosting that year's Olympics. Upon reaching the host country, the torch is successively passed from one set of hands to the next in what is called the Torch Relay. Typically completed on foot, the Torch Relay often tours throughout the host country by way of honorary torchbearers until finally entering the Olympic Stadium, where it is used to light the Olympic cauldron—a flame that burns until the closing of the games.[90]

Encapsulating an inspiring journey, the Torch Relay is a powerful image for understanding one of Jesus's final commands. Located in Matthew 28:18–20, Jesus is recorded as having appeared to His disciples, declaring, "All authority in heaven and on earth has been given to me. Go therefore and make disciples of all nations, baptizing them in the name of the Father and of the Son and of the Holy Spirit, teaching them to observe all that I have commanded you."

Contained in these three short verses is the method given to believers by which God has chosen to advance His kingdom—through disciple-making. It's no coincidence then that this is the same approach Jesus took during His ministry on earth. Choosing twelve men, Jesus poured into their lives for three years by teaching, caring for, and serving them. When He left, Jesus instructed them to do the same.

You can know that Jesus's disciples obeyed this command because the gospel of Jesus and His many teachings have come to you—having faithfully been passed down through the centuries, one generation to the next. Recognizing this relay of disciple-making should ignite in you a flame that is ready to burn brightly, and it leads us to how this topic connects with you.

Much as the Olympic torch requires the efforts of one individual handing the torch to the next, the gospel of Jesus and His many teachings have been handed to you with the same responsibility—to hand them down to the next generation. Although you are called to fulfill the command of disciple-making throughout your life, various seasons will provide unique opportunities to obey this command. With the close of your high school sports career, you have entered one of those seasons.

APPLICATION:

Your days as a high school athlete may be finished, but now it's time to pass along the lessons of faith you've learned to the next generation of high school athletes. Pick an incoming freshman to begin meeting with regularly. Use the time you spend together to intentionally teach, care for, and serve this younger athlete. If he or she is not a follower of Christ, the goal of this relationship will be to share the gospel with them through both your words and actions. If he or she is a follower of Christ, your goal will be to help encourage growth in the person's relationship with God.

TIP:

If you're headed to college in a different location than the younger athlete, you may find that utilizing a video call platform will be most effective for staying connected from your different locations.

OTHER

Committing to a College 175

Feeling Disconnected from God 177

Out with an Injury 179

Enduring Suffering 181

Contacted by a College 183

Winning the Fight Against Sin 185

Hurt by Christian Hypocrisy 187

Dealing with Shame 189

Preparing for the Future 191

The Week of State 193

Hopeless Against Sin 195

Doubting Your Salvation 197

During Spirit Week 199

Clarifying Your View of Eternity 201

Growing In the Fear of God 203

Your Plans Fell Apart 205

After Hearing a Sermon 207

Facing a Personal Problem 209

Life Seems Out of Control 211

COMMITTING TO A COLLEGE

This was it. T. J. had made it. With years of hard work and dedication behind him, the high school junior sat proudly behind a plastic folding table, beaming with a mix of excitement and nervousness. Looking around, he tried to take it all in. To his left was a bright orange basketball—one of his favorite sights. On his right was a fresh jersey with his last name stitched on it. Most important of all was the piece of white paper placed directly in front of him with the Georgia Bulldogs logo fitted at the top. Today was signing day, and having chosen to attend his dream school, all T. J. needed to do was sign on the dotted line. Drawing a deep breath, T. J. picked up the pen and inked his name. He was committed.

Signing day can be an exciting and sometimes scary experience for any high school athlete. It celebrates years of hard work and marks an important step in his or her future as an athlete. Committing to a college is a big decision, and it parallels a similarly big decision that Jesus taught about throughout the gospels.

We find this decision spoken of in Luke 9:23–24: "If anyone would come after me, let him deny himself and take up his cross daily and follow me. For whoever would save his life will lose it, but whoever loses his life for my sake will save it." In these two short verses Jesus is teaching a life-altering truth. When you choose to follow Him, you are committed. Jesus further clarified this point later in Luke 9:62 when He said, "No one who puts his hand to the plow and looks back is fit for the kingdom of God." Once again, these were serious words coming out of the mouth of the Savior, and they make clear you can't be halfway committed to Jesus.

When a high school athlete commits to a future college, he or she is making the decision to go all in. In these passages Jesus taught a similar point. Anyone who calls Jesus Lord is going all in. That means if you're a Christian, you've already signed on the dotted line. Conveniently, this mindset can be easily forgotten, which is why you must continually remind yourself of what you've chosen as a follower of Jesus.

Every day you make countless decisions, but each of those decisions should ultimately be influenced by one main thing: your commitment to Jesus.

APPLICATION:

Grab a piece of paper and something to write with. Divide the paper into halves and write "Jesus" at the top of one side and "Me" at the top of the other. Underneath the "Jesus" heading, list areas of your life in which you believe you have fully committed to God, and underneath the "Me" heading, list areas you believe you may still be holding back. Once you've finished, pick one or two of the items listed under the "Me" heading to focus on fully committing to Jesus.

TIP:

Find a Christian friend who can help you stay accountable as you work to surrender more areas of your life to Jesus.

FEELING DISCONNECTED FROM GOD

As Sarah entered high school, everyone in the Rocky Mountain High area thought she would be the next national basketball star. She wasn't just good; she was outstanding, and the press had picked up on it. With a significant height advantage over most other girls and a ball-handling ability unheard of for a player down low, Sarah's potential was through the roof. In fact, Sarah had already been receiving looks from D1 schools after her exceptional performances on her middle school summer league team. But there was a problem with Sarah's game that no one anticipated. Even though she was the most athletically talented of all her teammates, she was rather shy.

Although this personality trait didn't affect her skill, it became increasingly detrimental to her relationship with her coach. When Sarah had a question about a play, she was afraid to ask. After poor performances, she would leave the locker room without a word. Sadly, Sarah became so detached from her coach throughout her four years of high school that she faded into the background. With mediocre stats and a poor athlete-coach relationship, Sarah graduated from Rocky Mountain High with only a few junior college offers and ultimately decided not to play college basketball.

This story points out the importance of communication, a topic that is clearly covered in the Scriptures. If we look to the New Testament, we can find three simple words that speak on this point in 1 Thessalonians 5:17. They say, "Pray without ceasing." The command is simple, but let's unpack it a bit more.

This verse is not saying that God wants you to pray twenty-four-seven, three-six-five; that would be an impossible task for anyone. Instead, it's teaching that God wants you to stay in continual conversation with Him throughout the day. Here's a simple way to think about this.

When you have a text conversation with your friend, you send a text and then he or she responds. After that, you respond to your friend's text, and the cycle continues. To "pray without ceasing" works in a similar way. Maybe you set aside five minutes to pray after you get up, thirty seconds to pray before you eat lunch, and ten minutes before bed. You might even have a spontaneous prayer in the middle of the day.

Much like Sarah needed to communicate with her coach to reach her fullest potential as an athlete, you need to communicate with your Coach, God, to reach your fullest potential as a Christian. Continual communication with Him throughout the day is essential for a thriving relationship.

APPLICATION:

Think for a moment about how much you have talked with God over the past week. Do you think God hears from you as much as He would like? Find a time this evening to think through your schedule on a typical weekday. Identify specific breaks throughout your day that would provide a good opportunity to communicate with God and then make plans to do so.

TIP:

You may find it helpful to consider prayer from the perspective of what it accomplishes rather than as a duty to perform. For example, you might think *I get to talk with God* instead of *I need to pray.*

OUT WITH AN INJURY

The stakes couldn't have been higher. It was July 23, 1996, and United States gymnast Kerri Strug was preparing for her final vault in the team competition. With Team USA clinging to a narrow lead over the second-place Russians, hopes for Team USA to claim their first-ever gold medal in the team competition appeared to rest squarely on Strug's shoulders. Having had prior experience on the Olympic stage, Kerri might have been the ideal pick for the crucial vault if it hadn't been for a major complication that had arisen earlier in the competition.[91]

Due to an awkward landing in a prior vault, Kerri had sustained a lower-leg injury that left her hobbling with a lame leg. Initially hesitant about the idea of vaulting again, when Kerri was made aware of the importance of her final vault, she determined that she would rally through the pain to make an attempt.[92]

With her eyes locked straight ahead, Kerri accelerated down the runway and launched herself onto the stringboard, flying into the air. The Georgia Dome watched in awe as she completed her combination of twists and flips and braced for the decisive landing on her injured leg. *Smack!* Kerri landed cleanly and threw her arms into the air—a noticeable grimace on her face. After being carried off the mat, time appeared to stop until Kerri's score was displayed: 9.712. She had done it! Team USA clinched the gold.[93]

The story of Kerri's 1996 Olympic team victory serves as an inspirational example of a simple truth: every part of the body matters—a concept we find throughout the Scriptures. Beginning in Romans 12:4–5, we read, "For as in one body we have many members, and the members do not all have the same function, so we, though many, are one body in Christ, and individually members one of another." In other words, when you became a Christian you were included as one part of a bigger body—the body of Christ. This theme is continued in 1 Corinthians 12:18–21, which explains, "But as it is, God arranged the members in the body, each one of them, as he chose. If all were a single member, where would the body be? As it is, there are many parts, yet one body. The eye cannot say to the hand, 'I have no need of you,' nor again the head to the feet, 'I have no need of you.'" Practically speaking, these verses convey the message that as a member of Christ's body, you need fellow Christians and they need you. Typically, this need for community is fulfilled within a local church. Without even one member's fellowship, the body is weakened. That reality recalls to mind the story of Kerri.

When Strug opted to compete on her injured leg in the Olympic vault, she was clearly at a disadvantage. In like manner, when the body of Christ misses out on your participation in regular fellowship, both you and the body are at a disadvantage. Although, like Kerri, God's kingdom will be able to overcome such a disadvantage victoriously, when you are the lame leg in the body of Christ, you not only miss out on the beauty of playing a part in God's kingdom advancing work but weaken your own walk with Christ as well.

APPLICATION:

Do you have a home church? If you do, great! Make an extra effort to speak with your pastor this Sunday about ways to become more involved. If you don't have a family of believers you meet with regularly, find a fellow Christian you trust and ask if he or she has any recommendations for churches in your area.

TIP:

If you're having trouble finding a church that meets your preferences, remember that God's primary concern is for you to surround yourself with others who love Jesus and preach God's Word, not with the style of worship or size of the building.

ENDURING SUFFERING

In 2018 one of the most influential bodybuilders of all time,[94] Arnold Schwarzenegger, gave a motivational speech that received over 100 million views.[95] In the speech Arnold captivated his audience with these words:

> So, people always [asked] me when they saw me in the gym in the pumping iron days, they [would] say, why is it that you're working out so hard? Five hours a day, six hours a day, and you [always have] a smile on your face. The others are working out just as hard as you do, and they look sour in the face. Why is that? And I told people all the time because, to me, I am shooting for a goal. In front of me is the Mr. Universe title. So, every rep that I do gets me closer to accomplishing the goal to make this goal, this vision, turn into reality. Every single set that I do.[96]

Revealed in Schwarzenegger's words is the inner mind of a man who singlehandedly changed the sport of bodybuilding. Although he offers no reference to God, Schwarzenegger's rather uncommon perspective toward pain and suffering is unquestionably similar to an especially challenging attitude taught within the Scriptures. It's found in James 1:2–4, where we read, "Count it all joy, my brothers, when you meet trials of various kinds, for you know that the testing of your faith produces steadfastness. And let steadfastness have its full effect, that you may be perfect and complete, lacking in nothing."

The message of these verses is undeniably clear. As Christians, we are called to consider difficulties as a joy. Unfortunately, when going through a trial it can often seem much easier to take up an attitude of anger and bitterness toward God rather than following James's instructions. However, before we allow ourselves to surrender to that mindset, let's consider how these verses relate to Schwarzenegger's words.

Much as Arnold attributed his growth and success as a bodybuilder to his joyful suffering, Christian growth and success depend heavily on having the right attitude toward suffering. The key to maintaining this attitude is realizing that joy is not found in the suffering itself—even Schwarzenegger expressed that—but in what the suffering is accomplishing. Although delighting in suffering is a rather uncommon mindset to have, it's the very mindset that set Schwarzenegger apart throughout his bodybuilding career, and it's the same mindset that will set you apart from the world as a follower of Christ.

APPLICATION:

Take a moment to reread James 1:2–4. As you read the words, look specifically for the reason James tells believers to "count it all joy" when they face trials. Once you've finished, see if you can finish this sentence: "Suffering is beneficial for me because . . ."

TIP:

Check out the following verses for more reasons that suffering is beneficial for your life as a Christian: Matthew 5:10–12; Romans 5:1–5; and 1 Peter 1:6–7.

CONTACTED BY A COLLEGE

When Emma rushed into her coach's office, she could barely contain herself. "Guess what, Coach!" she blurted out. Before her coach had a chance to respond, Emma was already at his desk, proudly displaying her phone with two outstretched arms. Tears began to drip down her face. "Can you believe it? This is from Alabama. Like, *the* Alabama!"

After squinting at the screen for a few moments, Emma's coach's eyes widened, and his eyebrows rose. "Wow! Congratulations. That's very exciting."

"I wanted you to be the first to know. Now I have to tell all my friends, my family, my neighbors, and oh, I can't forget to post this on social media. . . . Coach, maybe you could even start having me announced first in the lineup. This is great!" Emma skipped out of the coach's office with a smile from ear to ear.

As she reached the door, her coach gently called out to her. "Hey, Emma—could you please come back here for a minute?"

Cheerfully Emma turned around and skipped back to her coach. "Sure thing, Coach. What's up?" She was bubbling with enthusiasm.

"I want you to enjoy this moment, and I know how hard you have worked for this, but I want to make sure you're seeing this the right way," Emma's coach said with a pause. "Simply because a college coach contacted you doesn't make you more important than the other girls who have worked just as hard as you, and it doesn't change who you are as a person either. I want you to be excited, but I don't want you to be proud."

Emma stared blankly at her coach for a few seconds before it clicked. "You know what, Coach? You're right. This is great, but when it comes down to it, it's only a message. Thanks for reminding me of that." After exchanging smiles, Emma left the office as enthusiastic as she was before, but this time with a slightly different perspective on things.

Hopefully this story helps you realize something crucial: pride distorts your perspective. That's why Proverbs 11:2 stresses humility: "When pride comes, then comes disgrace, but with the humble is wisdom." Notice the simple connection this verse makes. Wisdom is found with humility because it allows you to see things accurately. Pride, on the other hand, distorts your perspective and causes you to see things with yourself primarily in view.

It can often be helpful as believers to take a step back and ensure we're thinking about things correctly. In Emma's case, when she received interest from a college, she incorrectly saw it as an opportunity to promote herself. In your own life this can extend to many other areas. Pride is an easy trap to fall into, so when you're contacted by a college coach or have succeeded in any other way through your sport, enjoy the accomplishment. But remember to see it the right way—with the wisdom of humility.

APPLICATION:

For a real-life example of pride's blinding effect, check out the story of King Uzziah found in 2 Chronicles 26. As you read the story, look specifically for the different ways the king acted before and after becoming proud. These differences reveal key principles for avoiding pride.

TIP:

If you're looking for a story of someone who displays humility, Daniel (specifically Daniel 2) provides a great example.

WINNING THE FIGHT AGAINST SIN

On October 26, 1970, boxing legend Muhammad Ali entered the ring for the first time in three and a half years. Despite his time away, Ali was returning to the sport after coming off one of the most demanding training bouts of his entire career. Having settled on Jerry Quarry, an up-and-coming twenty-five-year-old boxer,[97] as his first opponent back, Ali was at it again, disciplining himself more than ever.

A biography of the legend would go on to later depict the radical mindset undertaken by Ali at this time in his life: "[Ali] went to work, doing what he did best. . . . He said he was running hard, sacrificing more, [all to be] sure he would make no mistakes in preparing."[98] As Ali stepped into the ring on the night of his return, he prepared himself for one of the most historic fights of his career. The bell sounded, gloves pounded, and after three grueling rounds, Ali claimed victory.[99]

When world-famous boxer Muhammad Ali returned to boxing in this 1970 fight, he exemplified what it means to have a radical mindset when it comes to facing a human opponent. This radical thinking exemplifies the same mindset you must have in facing your far-greater opponent: sin.

In the book of Romans Paul speaks of this extreme attitude toward sin when he commands believers in Romans 12:21, "Do not be overcome by evil, but overcome evil with good." This verse may not go into the nitty-gritty of how to fight against sin, but it isn't complicated either; as a Christian, you are called to fight.

The theme of this battle is given further focus in Matthew 5:29–30 when Jesus said, "If your right eye causes you to sin, tear it out and throw it away. For it is better that you lose one of your members than that your whole body be thrown into hell. And if your right hand causes you to sin, cut it off and throw it away. For it is better that you lose one of your members than that your whole body go into hell." Jesus's point is to take drastic measures when it comes to fighting sin.

Much as Ali took up a radical mindset to overcome Jerry Quarry, as a believer you must take up a radical mindset to overcome sin. Although Jesus claimed ultimate victory over sin on the cross, corruption will remain present until everything is restored. If you sit back and kick up your legs, sin will not leave you alone. Like any opponent, sin is set on defeating you, and it will only grow stronger the longer you avoid facing it.

APPLICATION:

What is one sinful habit that you are currently struggling with that needs to be defeated? Likely, what comes to mind first is the sin you need to face head-on. One powerful blow you can make to take down this sin is finding a trusted Christian who can serve as your accountability partner. The goal of this relationship will be to have someone in place who is committed to checking in with you regularly regarding your sinful habit. Although the thought of sharing your struggle with someone else can be very uncomfortable, don't let that stop you. The discomfort of a habitual sin is far worse than the discomfort of asking for accountability.

TIP:

Having an accountability partner is by no means a requirement for overcoming sin, but it can be helpful to have a fellow Christian holding you accountable.

HURT BY CHRISTIAN HYPOCRISY

You only have to say the name "LeBron James," and nearly any avid basketball fan would know exactly who you're talking about. Considered one of the greatest NBA players of all time, James has come to make jersey number 23 stand for a lot. Cracking the top ten in numerous NBA categories such as regular-season points, free throws, assists, triple-doubles, and playoff games, it's no exaggeration to say that James is one of the best his sport has seen.[100] With James's status in mind, imagine the following scenario.

It's a beautiful Sunday evening, and since you have some free time, you decide to go on a short walk through a neighborhood park. As you enjoy your leisurely stroll, a nearby basketball court grabs your attention. After a few moments of watching the pick-up basketball game, you cannot help but notice one player in particular who is embarrassingly unskilled at basketball. What sticks out to you most about this player is what he's wearing—a brightly colored number 23 LeBron James uniform, fully fitted with a jersey, shorts, shoes, and all accessories.

At this point you would probably think one of two things. Either *Wow—I can't believe Lebron James is so bad at basketball. He's lost all my respect* or *Wow, I'm sure glad I'm not playing on their team.* Hopefully, you can see the obvious answer is option two. Why would anyone think less of James because a terrible basketball player bought his jersey and decided to play in it? They wouldn't.

Here's the problem: this happens to God all the time. Often someone who claims to be a Christian acts out of line with Scripture, and those who see the unfitting behavior let it affect their view of God. This is the exact situation Paul was attacking in Romans 3:3–4 when he said, "What if some were unfaithful? Does their faithlessness nullify the faithfulness of God? By no means! Let God be true though every one were a liar." The point Paul was getting at was that regardless of how God's representatives act, it does not change who God is.

This same principle can even be seen all the way back at the very beginning of the Bible when Moses spoke to God. The encounter is recorded in Exodus 3:13–14: "Then Moses said to God, 'If I come to the people of Israel and say to them, "The God of your fathers has sent me to you," and they ask me, "What is his name?" what shall I say to them?' God said to Moses, 'I Am Who I Am.'" Notice God's precise words. God doesn't conform to who others think He is or how others represent Him. God is Who He is.

The lesson from these passages is clear. If another believer disappoints you or represents God poorly, don't let that change your view of God. That would be as crazy as allowing your opinion of an all-star athlete to be marred because of someone wearing his or her jersey.

APPLICATION:

An important step toward responding to Christian hypocrisy is understanding Who God is. Do a quick online search for "What are the different names of God, and what do they mean?" Once you've found a list, take some time to read through each name, noting the various characteristics of God.

TIP:

If you find a name of God that sticks out to you, try addressing God with that name next time you pray.

DEALING WITH SHAME

It was late Monday afternoon, and every distance runner on the Clydesdale track team was hunched over on their hands and knees. Nearing the end of a grueling hour-long practice, with the thermometer inching toward 100°F, each red-faced runner was dripping in sweat. To make matters worse, the team's rather old-school coach refused to lighten the team's workout, meaning that every individual runner was responsible to hit his or her goal times or would have to run again. Heat waves radiated from the track as one runner attempted to speak for the team. "I don't . . . think I can do any more . . . I need a drink."

"One more interval, runners," the coach replied promptly. "One more interval. Then you can have all the water you want."

This story illustrates a vivid picture of thirst. Extreme thirst. The type of thirst that is all-consuming and one that we should keep in mind as we examine the words of Jesus found in Matthew 5:6: "Blessed are those who hunger and thirst for righteousness, for they shall be satisfied." When Jesus said these words, He made a promise. Jesus promised that if you truly hunger and thirst for righteousness, you will be satisfied. How so? A few key verses from John 4:7–14 offer the encouraging answer.

> A woman from Samaria came to draw water. Jesus said to her, "Give me a drink." . . . The Samaritan woman said to him, "How is it that you, a Jew, ask for a drink from me, a woman of Samaria?" . . . Jesus said to her, "Everyone who drinks of this water will be thirsty again, but whoever drinks of the water that I will give him will never be thirsty again. The water that I will give him will become in him a spring of water welling up to eternal life."

Jesus's words in these two passages serve to teach a refreshing truth. Your thirst for righteousness is *not* satisfied by your own performance but *through* Christ's perfect life.

As a believer you might find yourself struggling with shame, moments when you feel on the inside the way the distance runners did on the outside. Discouraged and exhausted, you're on the hands and knees of your heart with merciless thoughts beaming down on you from every side: *You'll never measure up to God's standards. You're guilty. You don't deserve God's grace.* As you stare at the ground with the weight of shame holding you down, look up. The approval of God that you desperately thirst for has already been completed in Christ. There is no need for shame. If you have believed in Christ for eternal life, then God sees you in light of Christ's perfect righteousness.

APPLICATION:

The next time your thoughts cause you to feel shame, renounce the lie, receive the truth, and recite a verse. Here's an example:
Thought: *When God sees me, He sees a failure.*

- Step 1 – Renounce: I renounce the lie that I'm a failure in God's sight.

- Step 2 – Receive: I receive the truth that in Christ I meet God's perfect standard of righteousness.

- Step 3 – Recite: I recite the verse "For our sake [God] made [Christ] to be sin who knew no sin, so that in him we might become the righteousness of God" (2 Corinthians 5:21).

TIP:

The act of renouncing a lie, receiving the truth, and reciting a verse should not be seen as a religious ritual. The power of such an activity is found within God's Word as you remind yourself of what is already true.

PREPARING FOR THE FUTURE

"**B**e ready so you don't have to get ready."[101] Those were the final words that NFL wide receiver Marcus Peterson emphasized near the close of his interview on *Run the Day* podcast, hosted by Olympian Nick Symmonds. Peterson's punch line came amidst a conversation largely themed on the value of living in anticipation of the future. Although Peterson may not have been speaking of faith when he expressed this wisdom, there is still truth to be found in his words—a truth that Jesus taught in its deepest sense while here on earth.

The lesson came shortly after Jesus had left a dinner party with a group of Pharisees. Droves of people were flocking to Jesus, but amidst the chaos the Savior directed His attention to His disciples. As He began to teach, His focus turned to the importance of eternal things. That's when we come upon Luke 12:35–36: "Stay dressed for action and keep your lamps burning, and be like men who are waiting for their master to come home from the wedding feast, so that they may open the door to him at once when he comes and knocks."

In essence Jesus was preparing the disciples for His approaching departure and expressing to them the value of being ready for His return. This is the type of thinking that Peterson was tapping into, and it no doubt springs from his background as a competitive athlete.

As an athlete, when you begin a game the final whistle is what determines your attitude and actions. All you do is in anticipation of the outcome of the game. Your inspiration for the immediate is your expectation of the ultimate. In the same way, when you give your life to Christ, you officially become a servant, waiting for the return of your Master. As a servant, the significance you place on the final trumpet announcing Jesus's return is what will determine your attitude and actions in the here and now.

Practically speaking, Jesus is calling you to live every day in expectation of His return. When you have this mindset, the way you live will inevitably change. There is no time to push eternal things off. You must prioritize what is important—the things that will last.

APPLICATION:

If you knew Jesus was returning tomorrow, how would you live today? The way you answer that question will not be through your words but by your actions. Each day you wake up, you invest your life by the way you spend your time, energy, focus, money, and talents. Do a self-assessment by thinking through the following questions in view of an average weekday:

- What am I filling my time with?
- How am I using my energy?
- Where is my focus directed?
- What am I spending my money on?
- How am I stewarding my talents?

TIP:

If you're looking for something eternal to invest in, here are four categories to direct your focus toward: your relationship with God, your relationship with others, spending time in God's Word, and obeying God's commands (which includes serving God).

THE WEEK OF STATE

The words "STATE BOUND" were chalked in bright blue letters on countless car windows throughout the parking lot. It was the week of the state tournament, and the Little Valley Hawks men's basketball team had punched their ticket into the tournament. Throughout the school week, anticipation for the big game encompassed everything. The hallways were lined with posters, the lockers were decked out with goodies, student conversations centered on the event, and teachers were making congratulatory announcements to start class. Even a local media outlet showed up to interview some of the players.

When asked in an interview about the school's atmosphere as the game approached, the Hawks' star point guard described the scene nicely. "It's like this whole week has been one big countdown. Every day marks twenty-four hours closer to go time."

For many high schools, the setting described would not be an unusual sight during the week of state competition. Qualifying for a state tournament is a prestigious accomplishment, and the atmosphere of anticipation that tends to accompany such an achievement resembles an anticipation expressed throughout the Scriptures.

We catch a glimpse of this excitement in Colossians 3:1–4 when Paul relates to believers a thrilling truth: "If then you have been raised with Christ, seek the things that are above, where Christ is, seated at the right hand of God. Set your minds on things that are above, not on things that are on earth. For you have died, and your life is hidden with Christ in God. When Christ who is your life appears, then you also will appear with him in glory." Paul's focus for this present life was on one thing: eternity—and he's not alone.

The eternal focus that Paul encouraged can even be seen throughout the Old Testament. Moses's prayer in Psalm 90:12 is a fitting example, which says, "So teach us to number our days that we may get a heart of wisdom." Paul's encouragement and Moses's prayer reflect the same focus that all believers should have toward the coming of their heavenly home.

Much like the anticipation of state competition transforms the life of a student body, the anticipation of your next life should transform everything about your present life. The reality is that as a believer, you are living in one big countdown—a countdown until God creates a new heaven and a new earth. Every day marks twenty-four hours closer to this incredible event. The countdown is on. This world is not your home; you're "HEAVEN BOUND."

APPLICATION:

As you prepare for state competition and enjoy the celebrations that come along with it, take note of the significant influence one event can have on the words and actions of those around you. Use this exciting time to assess your own attitude toward heaven and how you might be able to apply the excitement seen around you to your anticipation of heaven.

TIP:

Pick a Christian friend to join with you as you strive to increase your anticipation of your heavenly home. Growing in excitement together will be more enjoyable than growing in excitement alone.

HOPELESS AGAINST SIN

Let's imagine you're playing in a basketball game, and you find yourself surrounded by a huddle of discouraged teammates, hopelessly watching your coach draw x's and o's on his clipboard. As you carelessly listen to your coach explaining his thoughts, the harsh "bbbzzzttt" of a buzzer startles you from your daze.

You glance up at the bright gymnasium scoreboard, only to remember that there are seven minutes left in the fourth quarter, and your team is down by thirty-five. This game is a blowout, and you're on the wrong side of it. You slowly force yourself back onto the court as the mumblings of your teammates fill your ears.

"It's just one loss. It's not a big deal."

"You're right, and there's always next game."

These discouraging words only intensify as you notice much of the student section heading for the exit. When you look over at your coaches for reassurance, you instead catch a glimpse of them peering down the bench and discussing which of the younger athletes they could put in to get some varsity time.

Impossible odds, discouraged team, hopeless coaches. If you're like most athletes, this is the point when you would give up. Unless there was a twist.

Picture yourself in the same situation but with one key difference. Let's say you somehow saw a glimpse into the future, and you're 100-percent confident your team will win. In that case, you certainly wouldn't give up.

With these thoughts in mind, let's turn our attention to a powerful promise found in the Scriptures that will help you see where this story fits in with your faith. This promise comes from 1 Corinthians 10:13, which says, "No temptation has overtaken you that is not common to man. God is faithful, and he will not let you be tempted beyond your ability, but with the temptation he will also provide the way of escape, that you may be able to endure it."

Through this verse God gives Christians an incredible piece of insider information that comes in the form of a promise. That promise is that you can always have victory over sin because sin is never the only option—God will not let you face a temptation you cannot overcome, and He will always provide a way of escape. Which leads us back to our example from before.

In the same way that you wouldn't give up in a game that you knew you would win, you shouldn't give up in a battle that God has promised you can be victorious in. When it comes to your daily struggles with sin, it might seem as if you're down by thirty-five with seven minutes left. Others may be discouraging you with their words, and in fact, those who support you may have given up themselves. But keep fighting; the only way to lose is to give up.

APPLICATION:

What is one sin you have given up trying to defeat? God promises victory over that sin, but you will have to place faith in His promises to see that victory. Next time you find yourself tempted to sin, remember the promise of 1 Corinthians 10:13. In Christ you have the power to overcome, so ask God to show you "the way of escape," and when He does, take it.

TIP:

Excuses are the quickest ways to self-sabotage your fight against sin. Try replacing excuses with "I should" statements. (For example, instead of saying "I will never be able to stop [blank], because I've been doing it for too long," say, "I should stop [blank], because Christ's power is enough to help me overcome it.")

DOUBTING YOUR SALVATION

Are you ready for some sports statistics?

1. In professional baseball (MLB), a typical batting average is .250[102] with the best average ever recorded coming during the 1924 season at .424.[103]

2. In professional basketball (NBA), a typical shooting average is 46.7 percent[104] with the highest career average by one player ever recorded coming in at 67.4 percent.[105]

3. In professional football (NFL), a typical completion average is 57.3 percent[106] with the highest career passing completion rate recorded at 68 percent.[107]

These statistics make it clear that when it comes to sports, perfect is . . . well, practically impossible. One hundred percent of anything is basically unheard of. Of course, this is no problem for most athletes and fans, who are able to enjoy sporting activities despite the imperfections. Although that might cut it for the world of sports, when it comes to having assurance of your salvation, anything less than 100-percent confidence is useless. Yet is that type of assurance even possible? And if it is, how can you experience it? The answer to both questions can be found in the form of a person, and His name is Jesus.

During His life on earth Jesus made a reassuring statement for anyone who follows Him. It's found in John 10:28: "I give them eternal life, and they will never perish, and no one will snatch them out of my hand." Did you catch Jesus's final words? No one will snatch them out of His hand. When you give your life to Christ, you're in Jesus's hands, not your own. Understanding that truth makes a world of difference.

If your salvation were up to you, then yes, you would have plenty of reasons to doubt. One misstep and things could be over. But when you recognize that Romans 10:13 really means what it says, "For 'everyone who calls on the name of the Lord will be saved,'" you can free yourself from the chains of crippling fear.

In the world of sports, statistics show that even the best athletes fall well short when it comes to being perfect. Thankfully, we serve a Savior Who is 100-percent reliable when it comes to assuring your salvation. If you humble yourself, turn to Christ, and call "on the name of the Lord," no matter who you are, where you are, or how old you are, God welcomes you into His family. The final outcome of your life is guaranteed because it's in Jesus's hands, and He never fails.

APPLICATION:

Set aside ten to fifteen minutes to sit down and write out the story of your salvation (this is called a testimony). To help you think through your testimony, consider the following questions:

- When did you place trust in Jesus for Salvation?
- In what ways have you seen your relationship with the Savior grow?
- How would you describe your current relationship with Christ?

Once you've completed your testimony, find time to share what you have written with a close family member or friend.

TIP:

Your testimony is about more than your conversion; it includes the work that Christ has done after your salvation too.

DURING SPIRIT WEEK

Caw! Caw! The sound of a bird echoed throughout the gymnasium as all eyes turned to see the commotion. There he was, standing in his usual bleacher seat, "Superfan Sam"—at least that's what the students called him. During his high school days, Sam served as the Little Valley Thunderbird's team mascot. Now, decades later, Sam's enthusiasm as a fan has only grown stronger. Easily spotted among the crowd at every home and away game, Sam comes regularly outfitted with an oversized Thunderbird's hat, bird-shaped facemask, lightning-bolt gloves, and a six-foot feather cape. As if his outfit weren't enough, he also rolls up to home games in his custom-designed 1990 Ford Thunderbird. Fittingly dubbed the "Thunder-Mobile," the car is decked out with "GO THUNDERBIRDS" decals and lightning-bolt-themed wheel axles.

You only have to take one look at Sam to know he's a huge fan of the Thunderbirds. However, what makes Sam of particular interest to us is his resemblance to a character found in the gospel accounts. This character appears in Mark 10:17–22 when he is seen approaching Jesus.

> *And as [Jesus] was setting out on his journey, a man ran up and knelt before him and asked him, "Good Teacher, what must I do to inherit eternal life?" And Jesus said to him, "Why do you call me good? No one is good except God alone. You know the commandments: 'Do not murder, Do not commit adultery, Do not steal, Do not bear false witness, Do not defraud, Honor your father and mother.'" And he said to him, "Teacher, all these I have kept from my youth." And Jesus, looking at him, loved him, and said to him, "You lack one thing: go, sell all that you have and give to*

the poor, and you will have treasure in heaven; and come, follow me." Disheartened by the saying, he went away sorrowful, for he had great possessions.

In this encounter Jesus exposed the tragic reality that someone can have an appearance of godliness without having a heart devoted to God. This leads us back to Superfan Sam.

Although there are certainly differences between Superfan Sam and the man from Mark 10, there's at least one significant similarity—their appearance. Both men appear passionately devoted to their causes. Both go to great lengths to make an outward show of their loyalty. But Jesus's response to the man in Mark 10 shows that the Savior sees straight through appearances into the heart. Jesus's command for the man to sell all he had and follow Him was a test of true faith, revealing an important aspect of the Savior. Jesus is not simply looking for fans who only look the part of being a Christian but for followers who also have a heart devoted to God.

APPLICATION:

A great way to keep your heart devoted to God is through private worship. Although worship can take many forms, one great way is through singing. Find a safe, isolated location and choose one of your favorite Christian songs to sing. If you prefer, you can also play an audio version of the song to sing along with. (You may also want to look up the lyrics if your memory of the song is rough.) Singing like this may feel uncomfortable at first, but remember: the focus here is worshiping God.

TIP:

Try not to see the practice of worshiping God through singing as a one-and-done activity. Rather, leave yourself open to worshiping Christ privately on a regular basis.

CLARIFYING YOUR VIEW OF ETERNITY

In 1996 an audience of mesmerized movie-goers sat on the edge of their seats, spellbound by the announcement of the up-and-coming film *Space Jam*. The trailer said it all: "When the world's greatest athlete, Michael Jordan, teams up with the world's best-loved cartoon character, Bugs Bunny, you won't believe your eyes.... Warner Brothers presents ... Jordan, Bunny. Together, they just might save the world. *Space Jam*. You've never seen anything like it."[108][109]

Attracting swarms of fans to theaters in the winter of that year, the hit film placed Jordan in an animated universe where his basketball skills were put to the test as he worked to save cartoon characters from a dangerous plot to take them captive by invading aliens.[110]

Attributed in part to the film's box office success was the creative initiative to mix a cartoon world with reality. This initiative has since continued to be a familiar practice on both the screens of countless movie theaters and, less recognizably, in the minds of countless people. The second of these two is where we will focus our attention, as it refers to the common habit of many to combine real with imaginary when it comes to the realities of heaven and hell.

Unfortunately, viewing things this way often results in a heaven and hell that look more like cartoon worlds than anything else. The Bible leaves no room for such thoughts.

In Revelation 21:4 we find an accurate description of heaven's realities: "Death shall be no more, neither shall there be mourning, nor crying, nor pain anymore, for the former things have passed away." This simple description paints a much different picture of heaven than the world tries to promote. Heaven will be far better than simply lying in hammocks and playing harps all day. On the flip side, hell is infinitely more terrifying than the world makes it out to be. Matthew 13:42 chooses these words to describe hell: "In that place there will be weeping and gnashing of teeth." This is not the version of hell that the world makes jokes about, but the place in which people will experience the real, eternal wrath of God. Hell will not be a place to party and ride motorcycles with the devil. It is a place of absolute misery.

The danger of having a cartoon perspective of heaven and hell is that it waters down the significance of eternity. If heaven isn't all too great, and hell isn't all too bad, it's easy to become unconcerned about your eternal destination, but think again. Combining real with imaginary may result in a successful movie, but it doesn't result in a clear view of eternity. Enjoy the movies, but leave the cartoons on the screen.

APPLICATION:

Take a few moments to compare and contrast the descriptions of heaven and hell found in the verses below. (See if they line up with what you expected.)

Heaven	Hell
Hebrews 12:22-24	Matthew 13:47-50
Revelation 21:1–7; 22:1–5	Revelation 20:7–15; 21:8

TIP:

Heaven and hell are realities that cannot be fully grasped with words. The descriptions revealed in the Bible simply use language we understand to provide us a glimpse of the eternal realities that will be experienced in each.

GROWING IN THE FEAR OF GOD

Imagine yourself in the following scenario. You're minding your own business, peacefully watching a sporting event, when suddenly you hear a roar of voices yelling, "Head's up!" Unless you have the privilege of being one of the many who are yelling the warning, you must act fast. You might look up, cover your head, or drop down and scrunch your shoulders. No matter what, you have to react. Nobody hears the terrifying warning of a quickly approaching object and remains unmoved. That would be borderline insane. Which is why this situation correlates well to the topic of fearing God.

When it comes to the fear of God, the Bible is full of teachings directed at both Christians and non-Christians alike. Though there is a range of lessons that can be learned as a Christian, there are at least two fundamental things to remember about the fear of God:

1. God is holy. "There is none holy like the Lord: for there is none besides you; there is no rock like our God" (1 Samuel 2:2).

2. Christians are called to be holy. "But as he who called you is holy, you also be holy in all your conduct, since it is written, 'You shall be holy, for I am holy'" (1 Peter 1:15–16).

(Side note: in the Bible, *holy* can be defined as "pure, sinless, upright."[111])

Together, these two passages bring a sobering thought into view: God is holy, and because of that, as a Christian, you are called to be holy too. In other words, you serve a pure, sinless, upright God, and He calls you to glorify Him by reflecting those characteristics in your own life. Understanding this produces what the Bible calls the fear of God.

It's helpful to clarify that when talking about the fear of God as it relates to a believer, this does not refer to being afraid of God's punishment. Christ has already paid for your punishment on the cross. Having the fear of God as a Christian is a healthy respect for God's holiness, which draws us back to the start.

When you're at a sporting event and hear the words "Heads up!" typically your attitude immediately changes, and rightfully so. When a flying object is headed in your direction, it's good to have a fear that causes action. Similarly, the fear of God demands a response. When you see God for Who He is—holy—you cannot help but adjust how you live.

APPLICATION:

The book of Proverbs has much to say about the fear of God and provides a great place to help you gain a better understanding of that fear. Make it a habit to start each morning by reading a chapter from Proverbs (there are thirty-one chapters in the book of Proverbs—one for each day of the month). If mornings aren't a great time for you, feel free to pick a time that better suits your personal makeup and/or schedule.

TIP:

Picking the same time every day to read your daily chapter from Proverbs will be helpful in remaining consistent.

YOUR PLANS FELL APART

When fifteen-year-old figure skater Kamila Valieva stepped onto the ice for her final performance at the 2021 Rostelecom Cup in Sochi, Russia, she stunned the crowd with a show to remember.[112] Smoothly gliding across the ice and elegantly spinning in the air, Valieva's performance was absolutely dazzling, leaving the announcers with only the highest praise. Tara Lipinski, an internationally acclaimed figure skater and Olympic gold medalist, remarked, "I'm speechless." Johnny Weir, U. S. Figure Skating Hall of Famer and figure skating analyst, praised, "Gorgeous! . . . This performance has been nothing short of captivating." And Terry Cannon, primetime NBC announcer, exclaimed, "Find me a free skate that tops that one!"[113]

This young skater's exceptional performance paints a beautiful picture of how many Christ-followers want and expect their lives to go: struggle-free, flawless living until they're taken home to enjoy the glories of heaven. However, this is not the same picture that the Bible paints.

In the Scriptures there are no promises that your life will go exactly as you plan it or that you'll be without any difficulties. In fact, the Bible promises pretty much the exact opposite. During one of Jesus's most famous sermons, the Sermon on the Mount, the Son of God said this about the life of faith in Matthew 7:14: "For the gate is narrow and the way is hard that leads to life, and those who find it are few."

Understanding this theme, the apostle Paul had something very similar to say. In Acts 14:22, shortly after being stoned and left for dead, the apostle returned to the city of his inflictors and was found "strengthening the souls of the disciples, encouraging them to continue in the faith, and saying that through many tribulations we must enter the kingdom of God."

When your plans fall apart, losing the proper perspective can be easy. This is where these verses come into play. Often followers of Christ anticipate that their lives will be smooth and elegant, like Valieva's performance. Although this might be a nice thought, it does not align with God's Word. If things aren't going the way you expected, it will be helpful to drop any unbiblical expectations and realign your view of life with the Word of God. It can be much easier to face difficulties when you're willing to embrace the truth that difficulties do not get in the way of God's plan for your life but are part of the plan.

APPLICATION:

The Scriptures provide numerous examples of how past believers have responded in the face of affliction. As backward as it may seem, in many instances those same believers would often respond with praise and worship to God. Although you might not feel like it, find a safe place in nature to take a walk, praising God as you go. (If people are around, don't feel obligated to express yourself verbally. You can praise God in the quietness of your heart.)

TIP:

Looking for a story that demonstrates praise in suffering? Check out the prison account of Paul and Silas in Acts 16:16–34.

AFTER HEARING A SERMON

Once upon a time two high school couch potatoes decided that they needed to join the cross-country team. The first said to himself, "I'm going to *try* cross-country this year." The other said to himself, "I'm going to *train* for cross-country this year." The following summer day, each woke up to his alarm, laced up his shoes, and made it to the morning preseason practice—a two-mile run. Struggling to make the distance, both runners immediately went home after practice and crashed in front of their TV exhausted. *Wow,* they both thought. *That was hard!*

The next morning they awoke so sore they could barely move. The first thought, *Well, I gave it a try. This running thing is not for me.* He comfortably slipped back to sleep. The second thought, *Well, this is sure hard, but I can't give up now. Cross-country lasts all fall. I still have a lot of training to do.* Slowly he moved his stiff legs out of bed and headed out the door for another practice.

As this story shows, there's a big difference between training and trying. Let's take a look at an explanation for both of the terms.

- *Trying*: deciding to do something without commitment. (It's testing something, seeing how it goes, and then deciding whether or not to continue.)

- *Training*: deciding to do something with a commitment. (It's choosing a goal and working toward achieving it.)

With our two explanations in place, we can now move forward in seeing how this difference can radically impact your Christian life.

Imagine you listened to a sermon about Matthew 22:39: "You shall love your neighbor as yourself." In your eagerness you decide to *try* loving others better. The next day your opportunity comes. After a team meal, you notice that the cafeteria is a mess. You diligently work to clean up the room, finishing just as your teammates return to the cafeteria. As you stand in the corner waiting for them to notice, you are surprised to see them walk in and out with no reaction. That's when the thoughts start to rush in. *Wow! I took time out of my day to clean up their mess, and they didn't even say thank you! That's the end of that.*

Now let's alter the situation. Once again, picture the same story, except this time you've decided to *train* yourself to love others. As you stand in the corner, surprised that your teammates didn't notice your effort, different thoughts fill your mind. *God, thank You for the opportunity to grow in love. Although my teammates might not have noticed, I know You did.*

Similar to the story of the couch potatoes, this illustration points out that you can hear the same Scripture and have two completely different responses. Why? The difference is found between training and trying.

APPLICATION:

Moving forward, make an effort to train yourself to apply sermons that you hear instead of simply trying to. One way to do this is by taking notes while you listen and then reviewing those notes later in the week.

TIP:

If you find note-taking distracting, there are plenty of other ways to remember a sermon (such as, listening to the recording, sharing what you learned with others, and so on).

FACING A PERSONAL PROBLEM

When the nonprofit Make-A-Wish Foundation teamed up with international sports channel ESPN, they set out with a vision to touch lives. Coming together to form the *My Wish* television series, the two companies worked together to take viewers on a series of powerful journeys into the stories of children with critical illnesses. Catching on film countless heart-touching moments, episodes would climax when children in need had their wishes granted as they met their sports heroes.[114]

Having touched the lives of numerous children, *My Wish* is a fitting introduction for a brief exploration of how being a child of God affords you the great privilege of prayer.

We'll start by considering what it means to be a child of God, which is clearly spelled out in the Gospel of John. Let's begin with the popular passage John 3:16: "For God so loved the world, that he gave his only Son, that whoever believes in him should not perish but have eternal life." The implications of this verse are incredible, and they are further explained in John 1:12: "But to all who did receive him, who believed in his name, he gave the right to become children of God." In the greatest act of kindness, God the Father sent His only Son so you could become a child of God.

Now as God's child, you have the privilege of asking your heavenly Father for even more good gifts. Jesus explained this in Matthew 7:9–11: "Or which one of you, if his son asks him for bread, will give him a stone? Or if he asks for a fish, will give him a serpent? If you then, who are evil, know how to give good gifts to your children, how much more will your Father who is in heaven give good things to those who ask him!"

Through the gift of salvation, God has granted you the ability to ask Him for even more good things in the same way a child does his father, which draws us back to the beginning.

What Make-A-Wish and ESPN have done in the lives of *My Wish* children is unforgettable, but what God and Jesus have done in the lives of all Their children is unimaginable. The greatest wish you could ever ask for has already been granted; God has given you the ability to become one of His children. Now as His child, you have the great privilege of having a Father Who delights in answering your requests. No matter what you face, never forget that.

APPLICATION:

Find an open space in your room, preferably on a wall or door, to use as a "prayer chart." With a stack of sticky notes in hand, mentally split the area into halves, placing at the top of one half a sticky note with the label "Prayer Requests" and at the top of the other half a sticky note with the label "Answered Prayers." When a prayer request comes up in your life, bring it before God in prayer, and then write it on a sticky note, placing it somewhere underneath your "Prayer Requests" label. When the prayer is answered, move it under the "Answered Prayers" label. (You can have as many prayer requests at one time as you would like.) Using this prayer chart can be a helpful visual to see the amazing ways God answers prayers in your life.

TIP:

God may not always answer your prayers by saying yes. Being a loving Father Who knows best, sometimes God chooses to answer prayers with "wait" or saying no.

LIFE SEEMS OUT OF CONTROL

Every year video game companies release countless sports-themed games, updating on the previous year's editions. As they offer their users an opportunity to enter into the big leagues, many sports fans jump at the chance to play these popular games. From the likes of Madden, NBA 2K, MLB the Show, FIFA, NHL, and others like them, these companies have found the secret to developing games that will sell, and it's no wonder what that is. Fundamental to the games' success is the element that the user gets full control. As humans, we like being in control. Except we're not. Although complete control might be a feature that sells video games, it's certainly not a reflection of reality.

In the book of Proverbs, Solomon exposed this delusion when he said in Proverbs 19:21, "Many are the plans in the mind of a man, but it is the purpose of the LORD that will stand." This is a terrifying thought for a nonbeliever, but for Christians there's no need to worry. We are reminded why in Psalm 46:10: "Be still, and know that I am God. I will be exalted among the nations, I will be exalted in the earth!" Nothing and no one will ever be able to usurp God's power. Simply knowing that offers great peace.

Unlike video games, where players have the ability to control what they see with the push of a button, move of a controller, or tap of a finger, these verses show that God does not operate according to our commands. Instead, as a Christian you have the privilege of being on the other side of the screen. By submitting to God's plan for your life and God's commands in His Word, you can be confident that God is leading you in the best way.

APPLICATION:

In a world of buzzes, dings, and constant notifications, it can be hard to "be still," but that is exactly what God commands. Pick a time this weekend to put away video games, social media, or whatever else might distract you to find a quiet place to be still. As you rest in the moment, reflect on Who God is and why it's a good thing that God's in control. If you're a note-taker, bring a piece of paper and pencil and write down what comes to mind.

TIP:

It's certainly not required, but finding a comfortable position to sit or lie down in may be helpful for you to rest completely in the moment.

ACKNOWLEDGMENTS

As I sit down to write these words, I can't help but think back on the past five years, considering all the incredible people, circumstances, and opportunities that worked together to make GAMEPLAN what it is today. From the God-given idea it started as to the devotional it has become, I truly don't think I will ever be able to fully grasp all that has perfectly worked together to bring GAMEPLAN to completion—but it can be explained. You see, these acknowledgments would be a complete failure if I neglected to acknowledge the God behind it all. Yes, countless people have spent countless hours working hard to bring forth this devotional, but . . . there was *one* God in the front, guiding the way. There was *one* God over the top, bringing everything together according to plan. And finally, there was *one* God from behind, pushing it to completion. Please don't take these words as merely a "Thank you, God, for blessing our work." No. GAMEPLAN is the Lord's doing, and everyone mentioned below (including this writer) has simply had the privilege of being used by God to bring forth what He already purposed in the publishing of GAMEPLAN.

With that said, there's no doubt that God used many talented Christians in various ways to make GAMEPLAN the most Christ-glorifying project possible. Each played a part that only he or she could, and for that I would like to offer my thanks. (Before I begin, I should note that the order of those mentioned does not indicate the level of impact on this project; that is something we won't be able to see in this life.)

First, I would like to thank my father and mother for the many ways they supported and encouraged me throughout this project. Although there are too many ways to include here (such as, helping provide space/time to work on the project, helping craft the title/tagline, offering writing suggestions, and so on), I am forever thankful for all the help they were as *GAMEPLAN* was being written. Furthermore, I would like to thank my brother, sister-in-law, and cousin Laura for the prayers they prayed over *GAMEPLAN* as well as for the encouragement they offered throughout the process.

In addition to my family members, I would also like to say a big "thank you" to Laree Lindburg. Although Laree is the only publisher I have ever worked with, I couldn't have asked the Lord for anyone better. Laree's patience as we waited on God's timing (when it didn't always line up with ours), her understanding spirit as I learned the ins and outs of publishing, and most importantly, her love for the Lord had a profound impact on the entire process—more than I can truly say.

As I think of Laree, my mind also goes to the numerous talented Christians she connected me with. A special thanks to Doug, the graphics designer, for his great patience as we worked to nail down the perfect cover design and interior design; to Becky Swanberg, the content editor, for the wonderful suggestions she made; to Lee Warren, the copy editor, who did an outstanding job of improving the manuscript in numerous ways; and to Jonathan Wright, the proofreader, who was a tremendous help in applying the finishing touches for *GAMEPLAN*.

Furthermore, I would like to thank Brian Smith for supporting this project from start to finish. From providing publishing advice to writing an endorsement, Brian truly showed me what self-sacrificing love looks like as he went out of his way for the glory of God. Alongside Brian, I would also like to thank Ryan Hall, who offered meaningful encouragement throughout this process, and especially for his excellent foreword.

With these two in mind, I would also like to thank Pastor Steve Crawford and Pastor Chad Eigsti, who served as the theological reviewers of *GAMEPLAN*. Both went above and beyond in their work, Steve reading the devotional more than once and Chad organizing more than seventy high school students to review the devotional alongside his work. (Thank you also to the students Chad used for the review.)

In close connection with the unnamed student reviewers, I would also like to specifically thank Noah Khokhar, Kayleigh Hamby, Grace Stiansen, J. Lindburg, Landen B., and Makayla Quilhot for beta reading the devotional at various stages in the process. Each of these readers offered wonderful insights and played a special role in making the devotional the best it could be.

Additionally, I would like to thank Abby Brandt, Emily Graham, and Brenda Moore, who allowed me the opportunity to spend class time each day throughout my senior year working on the project, something that would not have been possible without Roberto Ibarra, the then-superintendent of my high school, signing off on the idea; thank you, Mr. Ibarra. A last school-related thanks go to Kathy Rich and my former senior classmates, who spent time reviewing various devotions early in development.

Finally, thanks to Carrie Baxter, who allowed me to take time off of work to edit the devotional; this was a tremendous help.

For those of you who have prayed and/or are not mentioned here, thank you as well. I leave you all with these words: "For God is not unjust so as to overlook your work and the love that you have shown for his name in serving the saints, as you still do" (Hebrews 6:10).

ABOUT THE AUTHOR

With a burning passion for football by the time he reached seventh grade, Collin pursued the strictest of training methods, workout techniques, and diet regimens. But when his small Christian school failed to have enough participants for his middle school football team, Collin joined the cross-county team to fill this seasonal gap. It was an instant fit. Winning all his meets, sometimes by wide margins, Collin's love for running flourished. With his freshman year approaching, Collin knew he needed to make a decision since both sports occupied the same season. He felt he could not give his heart to two sports. It was either his first love of football or his newfound love of running.

Praying that God would give him direction, Collin felt as though the Lord gave him a clear answer to pursue running—a calling that Collin took to heart and continues to strive for to this day. It was a calling that took Collin from the highs of state championships to the lows of multi-year injuries. And it challenged Collin to come to grips with his true purpose in sports.

Through this process and by the grace of the Lord, Collin learned the true meaning of sports: to put first things first, honoring the Lord Jesus in every aspect of his life, both on the field and off—from practice to competition, in victory and in stinging defeat, and while on camera and while not. He wanted to represent the Lord in reverence and be His vessel for all to see.

Collin knows that in both victory and defeat it's not the outcome that really matters but our heart and walk with the Lord that we carry through the process. Collin wanted to live and compete in such a manner that when others looked at him, they didn't see his reflection but the reflection of the One he strove to exalt with the understanding that in doing so, we have already won in the game of life.

As you read this devotional and as you ponder these lessons, ask yourself, *Who do people see when I compete—the created or the Creator?* One always wins; the other seldom does.

—Richard Oswalt, Father of the Author

NOTES

1. Asher Chancy, "The 100 Most Clutch Moments in Sports History," https://bleacherreport.com/articles/506776-the-100-most-clutch-moments-in-sports-history.

2. https://youtu.be/0toCMwEBwLo [0:00:00-0:00:38].

3. https://youtu.be/O2cT6uTHcCs [0:11:05-0:14:04].

4. John Rohde, "Sooners Complete Three Peat, Win Seventh National Title," https://soonersports.com/news/2023/6/8/softball-sooners-complete-three-peat-win-seventh-national-title.

5. SI staff, "Opening eyes," https://www.si.com/high-school/2008/03/10/blind-wrestler.

6. John MacArthur, *Fundamentals of the Faith: 13 Lessons to Grow in the Grace and Knowledge of Jesus Christ* (Chicago: Moody Publishers, 2009), 21.

7. Rich Mueller, "Best Known Babe Ruth Autographed Baseball Sells for $388,375" https://www.sportscollectorsdaily.com/best-known-babe-ruth-autographed-baseball-sells-388375.

8. "Top 6 Best Sports Drink Brands," https://www.rookieroad.com/sports-equipment/top-6-best-sports-drink-brands-8208402.

9. https://youtu.be/rBc96uDKI8M [0:00:00-0:01:01].

10. Brian Metzler, *Kicksology: The Hype, Science, Culture & Cool of Running Shoes* (Boulder, CO: VeloPress, 2019), 219.

11. Thomas Dimitroff, "How NFL general managers draft: An inside look at the privileges, pressures and pitfalls of the big chair," https://www.nfl.com/news/how-nfl-general-managers-draft-an-inside-look-at-the-privileges-pressures-and-pi.

12. Ray Allen with Michael Arkush, *From the Outside: My Journey through Life and the Game I Love* (New York: Dey Street Books, 2018), 214.

13. https://www.basketball-reference.com/boxscores/201311230SAS.html.

14. https://youtu.be/6oYlb1-gglo [0:00:06-0:00:23].

15. https://www.basketball-reference.com/teams/SAS/2014.html.

16. https://youtu.be/6oYlb1-gglo [0:00:50-0:00:53].

17. "History of Israel: Timeline," https://embassies.gov.il/UnGeneva/AboutIsrael/history/Pages/History-Israel-Timeline.aspx.

18. https://youtu.be/VlbC8q4VkL4 [0:05:36-0:05:50].

19. "Jordan's Game Winning Shots," https://www.23jordan.com/winning-shots.

20. Joseph Delves, "What is the cycling Hour Record?" https://www.cyclist.co.uk/in-depth/cycling-hour-record.

21. https://timtebow.com/media/about-tim-tebow.

22. https://www.timtebowfoundation.org.

23. "Tim Tebow's Shocking Story About John 3:16 'Coincidence' Goes Viral," https://www1.cbn.com/cbnnews/entertainment/2018/january/tim-tebow-rsquo-s-nbsp-shocking-story-about-john-3-16-lsquo-coincidence-rsquo-goes-viral.

24. https://timtebow.com/books.

25. Steve Warren, "Tebow's Film Makes Top 10: 'Run the Race' a Big Hit at the Box Office," https://cbn.com/news/news/tebows-film-makes-top-10-run-race-big-hit-box-office.

26. Michael Middlehurst-Schwartz, "Tom Brady breaks Drew Brees' record to become NFL's all-time career passing yards leader," https://www.usatoday.com/story/sports/nfl/buccaneers/2021/10/03/tom-brady-breaks-nfl-record-career-passing-yards-drew-brees/5980054001.

27. Spencer Buell, "Tom Brady's TB12 Method Is a Best Seller," https://www.bostonmagazine.com/news/2017/09/28/tom-brady-tb12-best-seller.

28. Tom Brady, *The TB12 Method: How to Achieve a Lifetime of Sustained Peak Performance* (New York: Simon & Schuster, 2017), ix.

29. Ibid., 216.

30. James Clear, "Vince Lombardi on the Hidden Power of Mastering the Fundamentals," https://jamesclear.com/vince-lombardi-fundamentals.

31. David Kindy, "How Wheaties Became the 'Breakfast of Champions,'" https://www.smithsonianmag.com/innovation/how-wheaties-became-breakfast-champions-180978246.

32. Neil Amdur, "Prefontaine, 24, Killed in Crash," https://www.nytimes.com/1975/05/31/archives/prefontaine-24-killed-in-crash-prefontaine-track-star-is-killed-in.html.

33. Johanna Gretschel, "Top 10 Steve Prefontaine Quotes," https://www.flotrack.org/articles/5049085-top-10-steve-prefontaine-quotes.

34. Jacob Marsh, "How many watts does a light bulb use?" https://www.energysage.com/electricity/house-watts/how-many-watts-does-a-light-bulb-use.

35. Eliot Shorr-Parks, "How big is the Dallas Cowboys' massive screen in AT&T Stadium?" https://www.nj.com/eagles/2014/11/how_big_is_the_dallas_cowboys_massive_screen_in_att_stadium.html.

36. "How much energy does a World Cup stadium use in 2018?" https://selectra.co.uk/energy/news/world/world-cup-2018-stadium-energy-use.

37. Victor Mather, "Dick Hoyt, Who Ran Marathons While Pushing His Son, Dies at 80," https://www.nytimes.com/2021/03/18/sports/dick-hoyt-dead.html.

38. Rodrique Ngowi, "Racing helps Mass. father, disabled son forge bond," https://www.fosters.com/story/news/2013/04/11/racing-helps-mass-father-disabled/48963448007.

39. Sarah Lorge Butler, "Dick Hoyt, Part of Legendary Boston Marathon Duo, Dies at 80," https://www.runnersworld.com/runners-stories/a35866273/dick-hoyt-legendary-boston-runner-dies-80.

40. Julie Cart, "Texas Is a Perfect 34–0 as Longhorns Stop Miller, Win Women's NCAA Title," https://www.latimes.com/archives/la-xpm-1986-03-31-sp-2161-story.html.

41. Gary Putnik, "The 9 undefeated women's basketball national champions," https://www.ncaa.com/news/basketball-women/article/2022-02-12/9-undefeated-womens-basketball-national-champions.

42. https://www.blueletterbible.org/lexicon/g3528/esv.

43. https://www.theworldsstrongestman.com/events/atlas-stones.

44. Phil Blechman, "2022 World's Strongest Man Atlas Stones Results – Tom Stoltman Triumphant," https://barbend.com/2022-worlds-strongest-man-atlas-stones-results.

45. https://www.blueletterbible.org/lexicon/h1556/kjv/wlc/0-1.

46. https://m.imdb.com/title/tt0087538.

47. https://youtu.be/LerwIYmNFXY [0:00:26-0:03:29].

48. Carla K. Johnson, "Largest victory parade ever? An estimated 5 million celebrate Cubs' World Series win in Chicago," https://www.ocregister.com/2016/11/04/largest-victory-parade-ever-an-estimated-5-million-celebrate-cubs-world-series-win-in-chicago.

49. https://www.blueletterbible.org/comm/guzik_david/study-guide/2-corinthians/2-corinthians-2.cfm?a=1080014.

50. https://www.ineos159challenge.com.

51. https://www.youtube.com/live/k-XgKRJUEgQ [3:08:35-3:09:15].

52. "Eric Liddell: Greater than Gold," https://www.christianity.com/church/eric-liddell-greater-than-gold-11634861.html.

53. "The story of Abrahams and Liddell at Paris 1924," https://olympics.com/en/news/the-story-of-abrahams-and-liddell-at-paris-1924.

54. https://www.imdb.com/title/tt0075148/releaseinfo.

55. https://www.rottentomatoes.com/franchise/rocky.

56. https://rocky.fandom.com/wiki/Rocky_(film_series).

57. https://www.imdb.com/title/tt0079817/plotsummary.

58. https://youtu.be/thhYv6-Iz9A [0:00:40-0:00:45].

59. https://youtu.be/mUQMTFfewZc [0:03:13-0:03:16].

60. NBC Sports, "Michael Phelps qualifies for first Olympics at age 15 in 2000," https://olympics.nbcsports.com/2020/08/12/michael-phelps-2000-olympics-sydney.

61. Paul McMullen, "Phelps' swim opens eyes," https://www.baltimoresun.com/bal-phelps40219-story.html.

62. Thuc Nhi Nguyen, "The Check-In: Kerri Walsh Jennings shifts her routine to new Olympic timetable," https://www.latimes.com/sports/olympics/story/2020-06-14/kerri-walsh-jennings-changes-olympics-timetable.

63. https://www.fifa.com/fifaplus/en/tournaments/mens/worldcup/articles/france-1998-winners-champions-stats-statistics.

64. https://youtu.be/-jGfuLobBQk [0:02:16-0:02:31].

65. https://www.transfermarkt.us/aime-jacquet/profil/trainer/4160.

66. James Herbert, "How Kobe Bryant's 'Mamba Mentality' changed the NBA," https://www.cbssports.com/nba/news/how-kobe-bryants-mamba-mentality-changed-the-nba.

67. Tim S. Grover, *Relentless: From Good to Great to Unstoppable* (New York: Scribner, 2014), 227.

68. https://youtu.be/FaSy7j7zrk8 [0:05:20-0:06:05].

69. https://www.getty.edu/art/collection/object/103QSX.

70. https://www.khanacademy.org/humanities/ancient-art-civilizations/greek-art/hellenistic/v/statue-of-a-victorious-youth [0:00:14-0:01:12].

71. https://vimeo.com/323459636 [00:26:29-0:28:14].

72. https://members.usagym.org/pages/athletes/nationalTeam-Women.html?id=455257.

73. "Journey to the Olympics," https://www.bible.com/reading-plans/26669-journey-to-the-olympics/day/2 [0:01:13-0:01:23].

74. "Roger Bannister: First sub-four-minute mile," https://www.guinnessworldrecords.com/records/hall-of-fame/first-sub-four-minute-mile.

75. Martin Fritz Huber, "A Brief History of the Sub-4-Minute Mile," https://www.outsideonline.com/health/running/brief-history-sub-4-minute-mile.

76. Track & Field News, "The U.S. Sub-4:00 Miler's Club (Chronologically)," https://trackandfieldnews.com/u-s-sub-400-milers-club-chronologically.

77. https://www.merriam-webster.com/dictionary/competition.

78. https://www.merriam-webster.com/dictionary/opponent.

79. https://www.merriam-webster.com/dictionary/scoreboard.

80. "Don't want to talk about how disappointing it is for me: Serena Williams," https://www.firstpost.com/sports/i-dont-want-to-talk-about-how-disappointing-it-is-for-me-serena-williams-2431380.html.

81. The Secret to Victory Podcast, "Serena Williams: I'm Not Supposed to Lose," https://open.spotify.com/episode/7qL2YIjCJdUY6HHFRVQvwo.

82. Turron Davenport, "Music City Miracle turns 20: How it happened, where the players are now," https://www.espn.com/nfl/story/_/id/28441088.

83. https://youtu.be/FCJFmL4oxPE [0:00:00-0:00:36].

84. David Daniels, "Top 10 Trick Plays in NFL History," https://bleacherreport.com/articles/876142.

85. D'Arcy Maine, "Sydney McLaughlin runs 400-meter hurdles in record-breaking 51.90 seconds at U.S. track trials," https://www.

espn.com/olympics/trackandfield/story/_/id/31723464/sydney-mclaughlin-sets-world-record-400m-hurdles-us-track-field-olympic-trials.

86. https://www.instagram.com/p/CQrOX17h4Tg.

87. "The Eternal Weight of Glory," https://www.ligonier.org/learn/devotionals/eternal-weight-of-glory.

88. Tyler Brooke, "How Does the Salary Cap Work in the NFL?" https://bleacherreport.com/articles/1665623.

89. Andrew Brandt, "Business of Football: Understanding the Salary Cap, Dead Money and Impact of 2021 Decrease," https://www.si.com/nfl/2021/03/02/business-of-football-understanding-the-salary-cap-dead-money.

90. https://www.paris2024.org/en/torch-relay-history.

91. Dan Evon, "Was Kerri Strug Team USA's Only Chance for Gold?" https://www.snopes.com/fact-check/kerri-strug-usa-gold.

92. "Kerri Strug: The gymnast who battled through pain for a taste of Olympic glory," https://olympics.com/en/news/kerri-strug-the-gymnast-who-battled-through-pain-for-a-taste-of-olympic-glory.

93. https://youtu.be/Bwa5Bf656As [0:00:15-0:00:50].

94. David Robson, "A History Lesson in Bodybuilding," https://www.bodybuilding.com/fun/drobson61.htm.

95. https://youtu.be/u_ktRTWMX3M [0:00:23-0:00:32].

96. https://youtu.be/Px7bjMyPA30 [0:09:26-0:10:12].

97. Jonathan Eig, *Ali: A Life* (Boston: Mariner Books, 2017), 290.

98. Ibid., 291.

99. Ibid., 295.

100. Dave McMenamin, "Stats, superlatives and other feats: All the milestones LeBron James is approaching in season No. 19," https://www.espn.com/nba/story/_/id/32443207/stats-super-

latives-other-feats-all-milestones-lebron-james-approaching-season-no-19.

101. The Nick Symmonds Show, "Marcus Peterson, NFL Wide Receiver and Entrepreneur – Stay Ready So You Don't Have to Get Ready – 53," https://podcasts.apple.com/us/podcast/run-day-nick-symmonds-go-further-accomplish-more-run/id1381521821?i=1000446781401 [0:33:11-0:33:13].

102. "Major League Batting Year-by-Year Averages," https://www.baseball-reference.com/leagues/majors/bat.shtml.

103. Craig Haley, "Chasing .400: Who Has the Highest Batting Average in a Season?," https://theanalyst.com/na/2023/06/who-has-the-highest-batting-average-in-a-season/. (Statistics weren't always compiled the same way. Some would say Hugh Duffy had the highest single-season batting average in 1894 when he hit .440).

104. https://www.statmuse.com/nba/ask/nba-league-wide-shooting-percentage-by-decade.

105. https://www.statmuse.com/nba/ask/highest-field-goal-percentage-in-nba-history.

106. https://www.statmuse.com/nfl/ask/quarterback-completion-percentage-average-for-nfl-games.

107. https://www.statmuse.com/nfl/ask/who-has-the-highest-career-pass-completion-percentage.

108. https://youtu.be/oKNy-MWjkcU [0:00:00-0:01:07].

109. Elahe Izadi, "Twenty Years Later, 'Space Jam' is the movie we never knew we needed," https://www.washingtonpost.com/news/arts-and-entertainment/wp/2016/11/15/20-years-later-space-jam-is-the-movie-we-never-knew-we-needed.

110. https://www.warnerbros.com/movies/space-jam.

111. https://www.blueletterbible.org/lexicon/g40/esv.

112. Rory Jiwani, "More world records for Kamila Valieva in Rostelecom Cup triumph," https://olympics.com/en/news/skating-kamila-valieva-record-rostelecom-cup.

113. https://youtu.be/iCgWCChypBg [0:01:51-0:01:54; 0:01:29-0:01:31; 0:04:13-0:04:20; 0:04:55-0:04:59].

114. https://wish.org/mywish.

Made in the USA
Monee, IL
09 February 2025

11547886R00134